PERSPECTIVE *from* AN ELECTRIC CHAIR

To Jeanne~
Go Green!

Mo
Meuhardt

PERSPECTIVE
from AN
ELECTRIC CHAIR

MO GERHARDT

authorHOUSE®

AuthorHouse™
1663 Liberty Drive
Bloomington, IN 47403
www.authorhouse.com
Phone: 1-800-839-8640

First published by AuthorHouse   10/11/2011

ISBN: 978-1-4670-3612-2 (sc)
ISBN: 978-1-4670-3613-9 (hc)
ISBN: 978-1-4670-3614-6 (ebk)

Library of Congress Control Number: 2011917234

Printed in the United States of America

Contents

In Memory of

Louis W. Cunningham

"Pop Pops"

I picked up your nickel off the ground.
Now it's my turn to pass it on.

ACKNOWLDEGEMENTS

THIS PROJECT could never have been completed without the love and support of my family. Every piece of recognition I have ever received in life includes a part of them. So many friends have encouraged me over the years to put my life in writing; thanks for the push.

Thanks to Nick Marco for my initial manuscript evaluation and Geoff Pope for editing each line with a fine-toothed comb. Your comments gave me hope when I wasn't sure of my skills. Thank you to the whole staff at Author House Publishing for your work in making this project a reality. Rick Berkey, not only are you a wonderful radio partner, but you have become a great friend. Your writing skills are underappreciated. Thanks for taking the time to write the introduction even if it did mean having to take your foot out of your mouth. "A goal without a deadline is just a wish."

Mitch Albom, it may have taken me a couple of years to get you to a wheelchair hockey game, but it was well worth it. I'll never forget our first lunch together and your ensuing hug. Your kindness and wisdom I will never forget. Your assistance and knowledge is priceless. Speaking of hockey, Steve Nelson, it meant the world to me when you created the games in Toronto after I was injured in Calgary. The butterflies I had before starting was a once in a lifetime feeling. I never was able to have my dad as a coach, but you filled that void. Vern Mason, you took a young boy and let him explore in his career dreams even when you knew his passion would be sitting in a seat like yours. Lili Mina, you took that ensuing young man and hired him on merit and skills where others just saw four wheels.

Sue Arnold, you were the silver lining during one of my most difficult storms. Thank you for dangling a carrot in front of my nose, even when you were eating for two. To all of my teachers, thank you for not crushing the spirit of a kid who at times thought he knew it all. The love you had for your job has translated into success for me throughout my life. My fellow Trojan high school graduates, thanks for the love. I've never met another person with a disability who was so readily accepted and treated as normally as I was throughout school. What could have easily been the worst period in my life, turned out to be the best. You showed me that there is a lot of good in this world and the power of the human spirit can never be underestimated. Even though I may bleed Green & White my roots will always be Black & Gold.

Thank you to all of my health care aides. For the last fifteen years you have been my morning alarm clock and my goodnight moon. All of the beds you've made, messes you've cleaned and meals you've prepared have more than made up for the bleached clothes, coffee breath and tardy arrivals. The workers and volunteers at Canine Companions for Independence introduced me to a love and partnership that I can't put into words. Thank you for your time and commitment.

To the staff at The Ohio State University Neuromuscular Disease Clinic and Children's National Hospital, you have given me a gift nobody else could provide. The power of hope resonates through you and is felt by many. As long as you're willing to dedicate your life, I'm willing to fight the battle. To all of my friends whose lives were taking too quickly by muscular dystrophy, I will never forget you. The grace by which you lived your lives was honorable and inspiring. Muscular dystrophy didn't win. Now you are able to fly.

If a coach is loved by fans, it's usually because they have winning teams. Suzy Merchant, I love you because of who you are as a person. I can honestly say nobody has gone to bat or put as much of their own integrity on the line for me as you have. In many ways our story together has come full circle, but the best part of a circle is that it never ends.

Who knew that one fateful phone call looking for a daycare provider would lead to a friendship like no other. Kevin Sonnemann, words can't express how lucky I am to call you my best friend. My one wish is that your dream comes true and you'll be a high school teacher and coach. David and Jinny, the tangibles are numerous, the intangibles are infinite. Mom and Dad, I'm sure there are parts in here that you remember differently or you never even knew to begin with. My intentions were never to hurt but rather to be open and honest. You've each been my teacher, my friend, my shoulder to lean on, my physical care giver, my role model, my dream maker and dream challenger. You've been everything I've wanted and everything I didn't want at the time but needed. You are my parents and I hope I've made you proud.

FORWARD

66 **W**HAT DO *you mean he's in a wheelchair?"*

Those were my unspoken thoughts shortly before the start of the 2009-10 basketball season upon being informed I had a new broadcast partner as I was about to begin my third year as the play-by-play voice of Michigan State Women's Basketball.

True, I had told those who hired me originally that I would be willing to work with anybody they chose to eventually pair me with. But after two seasons in the role, there had been no indication that they were anything but pleased with my work alone and I had accepted that I was quite comfortable flying the plane solo.

It got "worse."

"Oh . . . and he's a family friend of Coach (Suzy) Merchant."

So now I've been told that not only am I going to be working with a guy who might not only have trouble viewing the court and telling listeners just what he sees, but who is also getting the position mostly as a favor to the head coach. Will this guy be able add *anything* to the broadcasts and will his physical limitations actually detract from *my* ability to do the play-by play?

One of my favorite expressions is: "Youth is too often wasted on the young." In this instance, God decided to show me that: "Blessings are sometimes given to the ignorant."

After working just two seasons with Mo Gerhardt, I am grateful that our creator decided to show me how fortunate I am that my own lack of knowledge didn't keep me from a great life experience—and a great partner.

Having done over 30 years of play-by-play at the high school, college and professional levels and having worked with countless accompanying analysts, I have learned the common ingredients in the "good ones" are preparation, knowledge of the sport, understanding of when to speak and (just as importantly) when not to and taking the time to assess one's own work objectively in a sincere attempt to improve.

Check . . . check . . . check . . . and check. Mo's work was off the charts in each category. I was as impressed with him as I thought I could be. Then we went to Traverse City.

My wife and I were proud to attend Mo's induction into the Traverse City Central High School Hall of Fame in the spring of 2011. At this induction, I was flabbergasted to learn that the phase of Mo's life I had been privileged to be a part of was merely the latest chapter in a novel that continues to get better. And the best part is that this "novel" is a *true* reality show. As you will read, how one person could do what he has without letting circumstances even slow him down—let alone stop him, is nothing less than amazing.

When we broadcast a MSU game together now, I can say that I don't give it much thought at all that my broadcast partner and friend (not in that order) is allegedly "limited" in what he can do. Don't talk to me about limitations. Actually you can . . . I can tell you dozens of my own limitations.

But don't even think about doing that with Mo.

In the middle of this past basketball season, a friend who the day before had attended his first MSU Women's game, commented to me that "I didn't know your broadcast partner was in a wheelchair."

His comment actually caught me off-guard as I had long-since stopped thinking about the fact that the chair I sat in had "legs" and Mo's had wheels.

I kept my instinctive reply to myself.

"What do you mean he's in a wheelchair?"

Enjoy the ride . . .

—Rick Berkey
Michigan State Women's Basketball Radio Play-by-Play Announcer
Author of *Morning Drive*

PROLOGUE

6:09 A.M. I look over at my bedside clock. Is she just running late? Has she over slept? Did something happen on her way to my house? Was there a scheduling error? At some point I'm going to have to go to the bathroom. I'm stuck in bed until somebody shows up. The sun isn't up yet, and my day already has added stress.

6:11 A.M. A key is unlocking the door. Eleven minutes late, but eleven minutes that remind me no matter what, I'm still dependant on others. Eleven minutes others can multi-task to make up—eleven minutes for which I must prepare ahead of time in case of situations like this.

6:12 A.M. My morning routine starts. After feeding and taking my service dog out to go to the bathroom, she in many ways performs the same tasks with me.

6:21 A.M. I sit up in my hospital-style bed, and she brings a urinal for me to urinate into. You learn quickly to give up your modesty when you have a physical disability.

"What pants are you wearing today?" I hesitate for a brief second before she adds, "Come on, Mo. You're supposed to know this ahead of time, and you're not helping with the time!"

I bite my tongue before describing a pair of khakis, as I want to add the reason we're late is her fault, not mine. The last thing I want to do is upset her, because of all I rely on her to do for me.

6:26 A.M. I remain in bed, and she pulls my pants up my legs as high as she can. My bed is positioned against one of the walls of my room, so when she rolls me away from her, I don't roll completely off the other side. With one hand positioned around my hips to support me, she grabs the pants with her free hand and yanks them up again as high as she can. This process is then reversed as I get rolled towards her and the pants get tugged up over my other hip. She then reaches up both pant legs and grabs onto my boxers to pull them back down into position; otherwise, I'd be stuck all day with them riding up my crotch.

6:31 A.M. I get rolled towards the wall again as she stuffs half of a sling under me and then back towards her to stuff the other half. It's then hooked to a patient lift that is used to transfer me from my bed over to my wheelchair, which is basically nothing more than a human crane system to transfer patients. Like a huge pile of rocks at a construction site, I get lifted into the air and then steered over to my wheelchair. After unhooking the straps of the sling from the lift, I have to make sure she doesn't pull the sling up and out from behind me too quickly or else I'm revisiting another wedgie and we have to hook everything back up and go over to the bed again.

6:34 A.M. She raises my left arm, and then my right and applies my deodorant. After my deodorant, she puts a fresh undershirt on me—over my head first, so I don't lose my trunk balance.

6:37 A.M. She yanks and pulls my prescription support hose up my lower legs to help with circulation and to limit swelling; the slightest wrinkle or twist will cause a sore or irritation.

"It needs a turn to the left at the heel," I tell her. "Pull a little forward at the toes and raise it at the top under my knee." I have to be picky and try to describe any discomfort, or else I am stuck for the whole day.

A pair of regular socks gets put on over the hose, making sure not to slide the hose up my foot as the sock is rolled and pulled up. It's hard not to feel like a little child as my shoes get slid on and then tied for me. I remember the days I could still do this.

"I'll put on the solid light-blue button-down style dress shirt," I say, in advance. She stuffs my left arm in first, then the more flexible right arm second. I simply roll the shirt tails up and inside my shirt, giving the impression it is tucked in.

I'm still not positioned exactly where I need to be in my wheelchair. I feel like one of the Three Bears from Goldilocks: "Somebody has been sitting in my chair!" On the count of three, I get a push on my left knee to help get my hips back into position; the same happens on the right knee.

6:46 A.M. After getting the sleeves untwisted and the shoulders and collar adjusted, I'm finally all dressed and ready for breakfast.

7:06 A.M. I finish my cereal and head back into my bathroom to brush my teeth. I maneuver a toothbrush around my mouth by bobbing my head left and right. I wash my face the same way after finishing brushing my teeth. Shaving also takes some effort as I lift my hand to my upper lip. I have a beard to eliminate cuts or other nicks. Brushing my own hair is no longer possible for me, as I'm not able to lift my arms above my shoulders.

7:15 A.M. Finally, I'm all dressed and presentable, but there is still one more task before heading off to work: my breathing exercises. I do ten repetitions on my machine, consisting of inhaling at a steady constant rate and filling my lungs for as long as possible. Just as in any stretching exercise, it's about being under control and trying to go a little further every time.

7:27 A.M. I have just enough time to sign her form, verifying she was there and then start my drive into work. It's a good thing I live so close to work or else I'd have to get up at the crack of dawn. Try explaining that one to your boss: "No sir, I'm not the one who overslept; it was my Personal Care Attendant. I was awake, but stuck just lying there in bed." That leaves a really nice impression and creates all kinds of misconceptions as far as my work ethic is concerned.

I've been up for two hours, but already it feels like it's been a full day.

What's your morning routine?

CHAPTER 1

TEN LITTLE fingers, ten little toes and a loud cry. Everything was normal as I made my first appearance into the world during the early hours of October 16, 1977. My parents, John and Ann Gerhardt, were thrilled to have their second healthy baby boy, Matthew Fox Gerhardt. Thank God, I wasn't a girl—not that I don't wonder what my life would currently be like if I was born a girl, but I don't know if I could have gone through life having the name Gretchen Ann Gerhardt. My initials alone would have said it all—GAG! Sometimes I wonder what goes through parents' minds when they name their babies. Don't they think about the ridicule children will go through growing up?

Even though I was born as Matthew, I will always have my brother, David, to thank for the name "Mo". He wasn't yet three years old when I was born, and the name Matthew was too difficult for him to pronounce. As hard as he tried, all that would come out was Matt-Mo. That being said, my future was forever plotted as my parents also started calling me Mo.

Sure, I've heard my fair share of "Where's Larry and Curly" jokes, and was asked when I was going to go "mow the lawn,", but the name Mo has become as much a part of me as other famous nicknames have for others.

Just as George Herman Ruth doesn't have the same appeal as Babe Ruth, Matthew Fox Gerhardt doesn't connect with me as well as Mo does.

My mom was actually grocery shopping when she went into labor. A quick ride to the hospital and a couple hours later, out I came. Dr. Don Good was the obstetrician. His wife would later be my kindergarten teacher—two early signs that, yes, my childhood, in the simplest terms, would be just that . . . good!

Both of my parents were school teachers within the Traverse City, Michigan, public school system. My mom took the remainder of the 1977 school year off on maternity leave, but went back to teaching the fall of 1978. That of course meant finding daycare for me. Through a friend, my mom had been advised to contact Bonnie Sonnemann, who had also given birth to a boy, Kevin, in May of 1977. Bonnie was looking to add a baby about Kevin's age to her daycare. It ended up being one of the most significant phone calls my mom has ever made.

At eleven months, you really don't have a say in who your friends are. It's simply whomever your parents take you to go play with. That's how it was for Kevin and me. We became friends before we knew we even were friends. Due to our looks, we'd never be mistaken as brothers, but I'm sure I spent more hours growing up together with Kevin than I did with my own brother. Whether it was building with Lincoln Logs indoors, making snowmen outdoors, or running around in our Underoos both in and outdoors, we did it together. After being together, just the two of us, a third was added to the mix a couple years later as Bonnie had another baby boy, Kyle.

Three is never the easiest number to play with as you always feel like you are one person short or have one too many. Even so, we always seemed to manage to come up with rules or adaptations to make sure things were even; for better or worse, that would become easier to do down the road.

I basically grew up with a baseball glove in one hand and a ball in the other. Sports are huge in my family, and baseball easily tops the list. My dad played all through his school years, spent nearly 30 years coaching high school baseball, and was the Field Director for the American Legion Junior Baseball program in Traverse City for 20 years. David was easily the top catcher in Traverse City, if not the state, for his age, and earned MVP honors his senior year on the varsity team.

I remember playing countless hours of whiffle ball with my brother in our backyard at 2206 Aspen Drive. My mom was a great sport as we literally ran permanent base paths into the grass. We always felt like we were professional players as we got to use some of the equipment our dad had for his teams. Best of all was our homeplate. We didn't have to use somebody's mitt, a hat, or any other odd toy lying around; we had a real home plate—at least to us it was real. It was a portable, heavy-duty rubberized homeplate you would use on indoor turf fields or with batting cages. No other kids had one, so we knew we had something special.

First base was the corner post of the deck that overhung the yard. Second base was a dirt patch we made by basically ripping out the grass and kicking the ground with our feet. After a few scoldings from Mom, I think she realized it was a lost cause when one day she found Dad helping us form our dirt patch for second base. It would turn out to be just one of the many things she would give up when it came to baseball and all three of her Gerhardt boys! Third base was a large tree that just happened to be placed perfectly to complete our field of dreams. The previous family that lived in the house had a fenced-in garden located in what would be left-center field. Rather than having to delay the game to open the gate and retrieve balls hit in there, this area became an extra outfielder. Any ball hit in the garden was considered an out, ghost-runners became a common term, and two brothers pretending to be the current All-Stars of the day was the norm.

I miss those days of crushing a white whiffle ball deep into the outfield grass with my giant red super-sized plastic bat, creating my own play-by-play call when it came down to the bottom of the ninth with two outs, a full count, and I'm the winning run. Most of all, I simply miss just being able to put on my glove and play catch with my brother, not because we now live in different places, have full-time jobs, or are too old for such leisurely activity, but because even if I did have a glove on, I doubt I would physically be able to catch the ball, and there is no way I could throw it far enough back to him. I'm a very positive and optimistic person, but lots of times it's those simple things in life I'm not able to do that get me down more so than the obvious bigger ones.

I don't remember the specific day I was told I had muscular dystrophy. There wasn't a specific medical examination that I recall. I do remember various doctor offices and wishing I had fish tanks with the same exotic fish. I'm sure my parents sat down with me one day and, in the simplest terms they could, explained why I was slower than everybody else; why I couldn't race up the stairs as fast as my brother; why I couldn't hit a baseball as far as my friends; why it took me longer to get up off the ground; why I'd tire out so quickly. I just don't really remember anything like that. You'd think I would.

In that way, even though I wasn't diagnosed until I was eight years old, I feel as if I've lived with muscular dystrophy my whole life. I can recall being in kindergarten and not being able to get up from the floor as fast as the other kids or not being able to pop up from sitting "Indian style" as it was called then. It bothered me, but I was about six years old; it's not like I was going to analyze the situation. The muscle deterioration in Duchenne Muscular Dystrophy (DMD) isn't painful in itself; and since it doesn't affect nerves directly, my normal sensations of touch and other senses were always in order. There was never a time prior to my diagnosis when I felt my body was acting in a matter that warranted telling my parents about.

I didn't follow the normal progression of most boys with DMD. From day one, I was considered an outlier. Normally the course of DMD is predictable. Boys with the disorder are often late learning to walk, which wasn't my case. Parents may notice enlarged calf muscles called pseudohypertrophy, one more symptom I didn't possess. Preschoolers may seem clumsy or fall more frequently and have trouble climbing stairs, getting up from the floor, or running. Although I wasn't clumsy, I did show these other characteristics. By elementary school age, boys with DMD may walk on their toes or balls of their feet with a distinctive gait. To keep balance they might put their shoulders back with belly out in a walk I have always compared to a fully pregnant woman. Nearly all those with DMD lose the ability to walk sometime before becoming a teenager. I was still fully ambulatory up until the end of my junior year in high school.

Luckily my lack of speed and strength at a young age didn't go unnoticed to my parents. With both being public school teachers, they had their summers off. In reality, neither had the whole summer off as they both worked other jobs to offset the lack of pay teachers receive. Even so, we usually picked the month of August to do a family vacation. I didn't have any other relatives that lived in Michigan, so every summer we'd usually pick one of my aunts and uncles or grandparents to go and visit. August 1985 saw us visiting my Aunt Leslie and Uncle Bill, along with my cousin Stephen, who lived in New Mexico at the time. They owned a motor home, and from their house we had planned to go to California to do the Disneyland/Sea World/San Diego Zoo experience. Along the way we went to the Grand Canyon and stopped in Las Vegas. Of course I was way too young to comprehend, "What Happens in Vegas, Stays in Vegas!"

My Aunt Leslie is a physical therapist, so before we took off for sunny So. Cal., my parents filled her in on some of the things they had noticed about my development. Without my brother and me or my cousin Stephen knowing the real reasons as to why, my aunt set up an obstacle course in their backyard. We all thought it was just for fun and something for us to do outside. In reality, she wanted to see how I performed with certain elements and reacted to specific hurdles. It was then, August 14, 1985, my parents' 14th wedding anniversary, that I received my very first preliminary diagnosis of having a form of muscular dystrophy—not exactly the best anniversary present my parents could receive. Unfortunately, it wouldn't be the last time bad news would arrive on that same date during my life.

I seriously doubt anything was said to me during the trip, but I sure do remember an infusion of doctor appointments after returning home. It seemed like everyone was with a new doctor, yet each had me do the same tests. Pull this, push that, sit down, stand up, jump, hop, skip, you name it, I was asked to do it. Each appointment seemed to end up with some sort of blood work having to be done. Even as a young kid, I was able to tolerate a high level of pain, so this never bothered me a whole bunch. Of course that's not to say I still didn't play it off as having to be tougher than I actually was and be a brave little patient. A sucker, stickers, Snoopy Band-Aids, whatever they gave out, I'd walk away with it for being so good. To this day, I still seem to have a way with nurses!

It was finally determined I would need to have a muscle biopsy performed in order to get a true and final diagnosis, at least as of then. The operation would be performed at the University of Michigan C.S. Mott Children's Hospital in Ann Arbor, Michigan, not exactly the first place a family of Michigan State University fans and alumni parents wanted to hear they had to go to. An exception could be made in this situation as we were dealing with medical issues and not touchdowns or baskets, as long as my hospital gown wouldn't be maize and blue. I also say "operation" as opposed to "procedure" because at that time the muscle biopsy performed required me to have full anesthesia, as opposed to just a local anesthetic in my thigh where the biopsy was performed.

It's funny the things you remember from certain events, especially those that occur at a young age. Once again, I don't remember any specific discussion I had with my parents about having to go and have an operation. What I do remember is the gift shop in the hospital and being able to get a collection of super balls that were painted to look like mini billiard balls. I remember being wheeled into the operating room on the gurney and bawling my eyes out when I got to the point where my parents could no longer be with me. I remember there was a large African-American female aide with me, something totally new for a boy who grew up in an almost exclusively white northern Michigan community, who said something to the effect that everything was going to be all right and she was going to wipe away my "crocodile tears." I had never heard that term before and was a little confused as to what she was referring to.

I remember waking up from the surgery and being told I might feel a little nauseated; I wasn't. I remember being told I may be nauseated upon being moved for the first time. I was! I remember when I got back to my room, I had a new roommate. All of his toes had been cut off from a lawn mower accident. I had always wanted to be able to use our lawn mower, but had never been allowed to. Cross that one off the wish list! I remember getting out of bed to use the bathroom, which surprised the nurses because they said it was usually too painful for people to be walking that soon after having a muscle biopsy in the upper thigh. But when you've got to go, you've got to go. After that, I ended up using a wheelchair around the hospital until I was discharged.

I don't remember exactly how long it took for the results to be determined and given to my parents. I'm sure they could probably tell you right down to the hour of the day. I can't imagine what it is like for parents to be told their child has a terminal disease and will be lucky to live beyond his teens. That's exactly what was thrown in my parents' faces. From having a healthy son that just seemed to be slower than the other kids, to all of a sudden having a son with something called Duchenne muscular dystrophy, which they were being told would take my life as a teenager—early twenties if I was lucky—was, I'm sure, a living nightmare. Shock, disbelief, guilt, pain, grief—there probably isn't an adjective that could fully describe their feelings. Diagnoses like that usually do one of two things to a family; it will either rip them apart or draw them closer. Luckily for me, I can't imagine having a closer-knit family than what I've been blessed with.

After missing my most extensive amount of school due to my biopsy since having the chickenpox in kindergarten, I was anxious to get back and see all of my friends. I was still in some discomfort, but able to walk around without much difficulty. Getting up from the ground was an even greater challenge, so my teacher, Mrs. Force, allowed me to sit in a chair when the rest of the class was seated on the floor. This was one of the first times I realized having a disability would have its perks every now and then! I couldn't believe how jealous most of the class was. All of a sudden instead of being the kid that struggled to stand-up, I became the kid that got to sit in a chair. That's quite the promotion in the world of a second-grader. Unfortunately, that only lasted about a week or two as I fully recovered from my biopsy and was relegated back to the floor with the rest of the class.

I wish I had more positive things to say about the clinic and doctors at U of M. Well, not really since they're still Wolverines, Michigan State University's biggest rival, but my experience with them was mostly disappointing, both personally and medically. My parents had a couple of run-ins with the doctors and never really felt comfortable or that their questions were being answered. Of course I was too young to be asking questions, but I do remember vividly the medication I was put on and the resulting side-effects. Prednisone is a common drug, used for a wide variety of disorders. It is a corticosteroid that works to treat other conditions by reducing swelling and redness and by changing the way the immune system works. Normally it is used for a brief period in low doses. It is also the one drug that scientifically has been proven to slow down the course of certain muscular dystrophies, but only when taken continuously and in mega-doses. The reason most doctors don't like prescribing prednisone is due to its many side-effects. It's been known to cause extreme changes in mood or personality, acne, sensitivity to the sun, thin or fragile skin, increased bruising, slowed healing of cuts and bruises, increased hair growth, changes in the way fat is spread around the body, vision problems, sudden weight gain, and swelling of the lower legs, among many other reactions. Prednisone can also slow or stunt growth and increase the risk of developing osteoporosis.

It would have been nice to know some of those things before being told to take such a large dosage. In the span of barely over a month, my weight increased by over 50% as I went from 60 pounds to close to 100 pounds. I went from looking like a normal boy, to looking like the next coming of Augustus Gloop from *Charlie and the Chocolate Factory*. My parents didn't know what to do, and we didn't receive any guidance from the doctors.

We weren't told it was vital to maintain an extremely low-sodium diet while taking prednisone. Most people should limit their daily intake of sodium to around 2,500 milligrams, but the average American consumes closer to 4,000 milligrams daily. On my dosage of prednisone, I should have been maximizing my intake at 1,500 milligrams a day.

The first time I realized I had turned into the "fat kid" was after coming in from recess one day at school. Our teacher would always have us sit at our desks with our heads down and the lights off for a few minutes, so we'd calm down after playing outside. I just happened to look up and saw one of the other boys looking directly at me with his face all puffed out and full mimicking my new set of chipmunk cheeks. It was then and there I knew I couldn't continue down that current path.

When we told the doctors of my struggles, they acted as if I should have known of the likelihood of gaining weight while on prednisone. It was just one more example of poor communication with those doctors and the last straw as far as seeing them. My parents took the opportunity to do some research and find the leading research centers for DMD in the country. As the saying goes, when one door closes another one opens. That's exactly what happened for us. The closest leading research center ended up being located in Columbus, Ohio at The Ohio State University. The Muscular Dystrophy Association (MDA) clinic was led by Dr. Jerry Mendell, the leading authority on DMD research in the nation, if not the world. To this day, I still see Dr. Mendell. I guess that tells you my experience has been much better with him compared to being seen in Ann Arbor. That's what I get for putting my faith in a bunch of Wolverines!

CHAPTER 2

I MAY HAVE been a Michigan State Spartan entering Ohio State Buckeye territory, but we put the differences aside and found common ground in despising the University of Michigan Wolverines! After an eight-hour drive from Traverse City, MI, to Columbus, OH, my parents and I had our doubts that a new clinic would warrant a return trip. Little did we know how many miles would be placed on our vans making future interstate trips.

Our first interaction at the OSU clinic was with Linda Signore and Wendy King. Linda was the clinical nurse and Wendy a physical therapist. Both were very nice, welcomed us, and genuinely seemed to want us to feel comfortable. It was a nice change from some of the other clinics we had previously experienced.

Of course, as with any first time patient, baseline tests had to be performed, so Wendy put me through the same strength and range of motion tests I had been through for what seemed like hundreds of times over the previous year. There was a difference though; Wendy was actually talking to me rather than just telling me to do this or do that. She was smiling and seemed to be happy, while the room we were in was decorated with fun posters; the whole atmosphere was different. Somehow it felt more like going through stations in gym class compared to being a medical lab rat.

My experience with Linda was more of the same. Whether she was listening to my heart or taking my blood pressure, she seemed to be more interested in finding out my interests. Once again, she was happy and enjoying herself. Weren't all people that worked at these clinics supposed to be grumpy and look at patients as work instead of individuals with feelings? She was actually apologizing to me for having to draw some blood. Here was my chance to impress my new friend. Did I just say "friend"? Yes, these people were actually becoming my friends. As Linda was getting ready to prick me with her needle, I started to act as if this was really a serious event. I bit down on my lower lip and squinted my eyes really tightly, making it look as if she was about to torture me. The needle went into my arm, and I didn't make a single noise or move an inch; slowly my eyes opened all the way, my lips returned to normal, and a smile came across my face. Linda was just amazed at how brave I had been and what an easy patient I was for her to draw blood from. She said, "It's such a struggle with so many boys and girls as they cry and move all around making it difficult to actually get the needle in the right spot." Once again, I won a nurse over by putting on my brave face. If only I could currently get a date or win a girl over the same way!

Things were just going too well for everything to work out. After all, we still hadn't met with a doctor yet. We had heard about Dr. Jerry Mendell, but nothing that had previously been said really prepared us for what we were in store for. Dr. Mendell can be a very intimidating person who has a wealth of knowledge in his head. He's spent his entire professional career trying to find a cure for multiple forms of muscular dystrophies and won't be satisfied until he does. I would classify him as a perfectionist, and he expects the same from others around him. Until you get to know him, he can seem a little harsh; in truth, he is one of the most caring doctors I have ever met. It just took my parents and me a couple of return trips to grasp that.

One thing we didn't have to figure out was how much more knowledge Dr. Mendell had compared to any other doctor we had previously been with. There wasn't a single question asked that he didn't have an answer to. Not only did he have answers, but he was talking about things we had never even heard of before. I think my mom left the clinic with a school bag full of pamphlets, articles, and notes; all of them were on topics my parents had desperately wanted to know about, but had never been informed of.

One pattern which had started with my previous doctor appointments continued with Dr. Mendell. At the end of meeting with a doctor, my parents always asked to have time with him or her alone. This was fine with me, but I knew the things being discussed were never happy thoughts as my dad would always come out of the office with blood-shot eyes and a runny nose—both sure-tell signs that some crying had just occurred. I didn't mind being asked to leave the room, as no one enjoys seeing their parents' cry, especially when you're the subject they're crying over. I also respect my parents for realizing some of the subject matter they were discussing wasn't appropriate for me at that age. I never felt as if they were hiding something from me or saying things behind my back. They just needed to get the facts and then as parents to determine in their own way how to share with me what was going on with my body and what would continue to happen in the future. This also gave me the opportunity to go back to the waiting room on my own, which had various handheld games to play with, so I wasn't about to complain!

After concluding that first visit, I would never have guessed how close I would become, not only with Linda and Wendy, but also Dr. Mendell. All three have and continue to play, a major role in my life. Our relationships have even grown outside of my clinical appointments as I now consider them my close friends.

From an early age, I let it be known that one of my major goals in life was to go to college and graduate from Michigan State University. Linda never let me forget that dream and made the promise she would make the trip from Ohio to Michigan and be in attendance at my graduation ceremony. She was always sure not to say *if* I were to graduate, but rather *when* I would graduate. I always thought it was a nice verbal promise, but I knew things come up; and after all, how many nurses would actually travel roughly four hours just to be present at a graduation ceremony for one of their patients at a school they have no connections with? Hey, let's also not forget this meant I would actually have to go off to college and graduate, both being two huge feats in their own right! Sure enough, come May of 2000, there was Linda with her husband, Art, celebrating my accomplishment along with my family.

At the time of my original diagnosis, there was still a lot to be learned about DMD. DNA testing wasn't readily available, and a diagnosis was made using more of a clinical method as opposed to a scientific basis. In diagnosing any form of muscular dystrophy, a doctor would usually begin by getting a patient and family history while performing physical examinations. The history and physical examinations went a long way towards making a diagnosis. Nowadays, the availability of DNA diagnostic tests, using either blood cells or muscle cells, has greatly expanded knowledge, resulting in precise genetic information. From a biopsy, a doctor can tell a great deal about what's actually happening inside the muscles. Modern techniques can use the biopsy to distinguish muscular

dystrophies from inflammatory and other disorders as well as between different forms of muscular dystrophy. Other tests on the biopsy sample can provide information about which muscle proteins are present in the muscle cells, and whether they're present in the normal amounts and in the right locations.

Not too shortly after I was diagnosed, one of the largest breakthroughs in muscular dystrophy research was made. Luckily for me, that discovery was specifically for DMD. In 1986 MDA-supported researchers identified the gene that causes DMD when flawed or mutated.

Science Lesson #1: The protein associated with the gene, called dystrophin, was identified in 1987. Using a basic elementary description, genes contain codes, or recipes, for proteins. Proteins are biological components that are very important in all forms of life. Muscles are made up of bundles of fibers or cells. A group of independent proteins along the membrane surrounding each fiber helps to keep muscle cells working properly. When a particular gene on the X chromosome fails to make the protein dystrophin, DMD is the result.

Due to how genetic diseases are inherited, DMD can run in a family even if only one person in the biological family has it. You may have noticed I have only talked about boys when mentioning DMD. This is because it is inherited in an X-linked pattern on the X chromosome.

Science Lesson #2: Boys receive a "Y" chromosome from their dad and a "X" chromosome from their mom. Girls get two X chromosomes, one from each parent. When a mother has a mutation on one of her two X chromosomes, there is a 50% chance of her son inheriting that flawed gene and having DMD. A girl would have a 50% chance of also inheriting that mutation and then becoming a carrier, which means she could later

have a child of her own with the disease or mutation, but she would have no symptoms of the disease herself. In a few rare cases, this ends up being a manifesting carrier, resulting in a milder form of the disease. Males with DMD can't pass the flawed gene to boys because they give sons their Y chromosome, not their X. Unfortunately, they always pass the flawed gene on to daughters, because girls inherit their father's only X chromosome. This still doesn't fully explain why females don't get DMD. In most cases, a daughter usually gets a healthy dystrophin gene from her father, resulting in enough protein to protect her from the effects of the disease. Boys don't have the second dystrophin gene to make up for the faulty one.

Both sides of my family were quite good in keeping records and having knowledge of my ancestors' health. There was no known history of any form of muscular dystrophy on either side. Blood work was done on both of my parents to see if my DMD mutation could be traced through either of them. I'm sure this was a nerve-racking process for both as they waited to receive the results. It's never been a part of my thought process, but to them I'm sure it was like waiting to find who was at fault for their child having this terminal disease. There would be no finger pointing, but I'm sure the guilt would initially have been tremendous. The results came back, and they were negative for both my mom and dad—not negative meaning bad for both, but negative meaning neither of them showed a mutation. This was just one of many cases in my medical history where I haven't fallen into the most common scenario.

So, how can a family with no history of DMD suddenly have a son with the disease? Let's continue our science lessons. **Science Lesson #3**: If a boy has DMD, and it can't be traced through his parents, then it is a result of a *new random genetic mutation*. This mutation would occur in an egg cell; and since that isn't in a mother's blood cells, it is impossible to detect. In other words, the mutation is just a random act or freak of

nature. Imagine being told my disease was a result of a mutation, right around the time period when *Teenage Mutant Ninja Turtles* was both a popular cartoon and movie. Talk about confusing images running through a young boy's head!

As with many terminal diseases, it isn't the disease itself that results in death. It is outlaying effects from the disease that cause death. The human heart is a muscle which can become weakened by a lack of dystrophin, resulting in cardiomyopathy, or heart muscle weakness. Just as the skeletal muscles within the body deteriorate, so does the muscle layer of the heart, putting boys with DMD at risk of heart failure. The muscles that operate the lungs and the diaphragm also weaken, resulting in a weakened respiratory system. This makes it more difficult to cough and fight off infections. Pneumonia is more common from a regular cold and must be treated promptly before a serious respiratory emergency occurs. As the disease progresses and breathing ability declines, assisted ventilation may be needed, either from a noninvasive device or later on from a full-time ventilator. A tracheostomy can be performed allowing air to be delivered directly to the lungs.

Growing up, it has always been a weakness or a complication with my respiratory system that has frightened me the most. I do daily breathing exercises to help the elasticity of my lungs to prevent them from not being able to expand as normal. Not being able to breathe or cough hard enough to clear a blocked object from my throat is a daily worry. Choking on a piece of food is something I take a concerned effort to avoid, not that anybody wouldn't try to avoid choking whenever possible. Being in a wheelchair and not able to stand on my own, having somebody perform the Heimlich Maneuver would be a very tricky proposition.

CHAPTER 3

THE LEGAL Eagles—to this day I still remember the name of my first organized sports team. Our colors were maroon and dark mustard yellow, not exactly the fashion statement most people want to be making. Fortunately, I was at the age where looks didn't matter. All I cared about was that I had a uniform and was on an organized baseball team, just like the players on my dad's high school team I had looked up to. Even if it was just T-Ball, I was going to be able to show my skills! I guess I can't really say "looks didn't matter" to me, because they did, at least when it came to trying to look like a professional ball player, not some ragtag kid. Our team sponsor, a local legal firm—hence the name Legal Eagles—provided us with pants, jerseys, and hats. That wasn't good enough for me; I had my dad take me to Dave Harvey's Athletic Supply to complete the uniform with my first pair of rubber cleats, white sanitary socks, maroon stirrups, and a batting glove. If I would've had my way, I also would have gotten a pair of flip-down sunglasses, eye-black, and a season's supply of Big League Chew to stuff in the side of my mouth to create that big shiny bulge like all the big leaguers seemed to have in theirs. I couldn't wait to put everything on and begin my trek towards playing professional baseball. I had my dad show me how to properly blouse the bottoms of my pants, so I could show just the right amount of my stirrups. I remember standing backwards in front of a mirror, looking like a dog attempting to catch its tail, trying to

see if my batting glove was showing enough out of my rear pocket. If I wasn't good, it wasn't going to be due to not being properly outfitted.

That season was the first of what would become many years throughout my life on teams with losing records. I'm not talking about just a game or two under .500; I'm talking about teams that struggled to simply win a single game all season! I was able to play organized baseball for three seasons, and I think my teams recorded a grand total of three wins. Remember now, over that three-year span we're talking about kids probably from the age of six through nine. You had some kids that knew what they were doing and at an early age were advanced in their coordination and development; but for the most part, everybody had close to the same athletic skills, especially compared to the older leagues when participants would start to specialize in a single sport. My first season as a Legal Eagle, we won one game; season two saw us double that total to two games. My one season in C-Ball, which was one step above T-Ball with live pitching for the first three innings and then coaches pitching the final three, went without a single victory. That team was even worse than our new uniform colors, bright red and tennis-ball yellow. We looked like a bunch of young recruits for the local fire department. Here's how bad that team was: a year into my muscular dystrophy diagnosis, and I was the team's top pitcher and second best overall player—behind a girl! Now I have nothing against girls playing baseball, and I previously and currently know of some that are great athletes, but generally speaking, when the best player on a baseball team of basically all boys is a girl, it's going to be a long season.

I really don't know how teams were picked in those days, but I've always liked to associate it with how drafts are set up in professional sports. The teams with the worst records get to draft first, so they naturally select the best player available with their first pick. A player who is a stud in college gets stuck on a struggling pro team for the first couple of seasons until it can pick up some other talent and improve. The last name of Gerhardt was known for baseball in Traverse City, so when my name appeared on the list of available players, it was snatched in hopes of finding a star to build a team around for years to come. At least that's how I like to rationalize it! My brother had done nothing but increase that belief as he was well on his way to being a summer league star. His luck was much different than mine, as his teams seemed to win the championship each year he played. I think there was only one season where the team he played on didn't either finish in first place during the regular season or make it to the championship game in the playoffs.

For most of the kids on my teams, it didn't matter if we won or lost, as long as a trip down to the local ice cream parlor was in the plans for after the game. Although I never turned down the ice cream, I still haven't forgotten about all those losing seasons. If nothing else, it taught me how to deal with defeat at an early age. I truly feel by being a member of those teams, I was helped later on in my childhood to deal with my disability and some of the limits it placed on my activities. I wasn't going to be able to throw a football the farthest, hit a baseball the hardest, or run the fastest times, but I wasn't going to allow that to diminish my determination and love for sports and life.

Even after my diagnosis, I wasn't about to let sports erode from my life. Once it became too difficult for me to participate at an organized level, my friends still found ways for me to participate in our own games. Whether it was through special rules early on that still allowed me to play, or by acting as the referee or official once it became too difficult for me to even utilize special rules to play, sports remained a part of my life. I even found a way to profit off not being able to play. Starting in junior high, I operated the clock and scoreboard for all boys and girls basketball games and continued in high school, primarily for volleyball. I also helped out with the city's summer baseball program by umpiring T-Ball games, the same league I had played in right around the period when I was diagnosed. These were all paid positions which ended up providing me with enough money to save for some of my college, collect baseball cards, and have a serious girlfriend while in high school, prioritized not necessarily in that order!

While in college, I came back home each summer and volunteered to coach various baseball teams. I figured C-Ball would be the best league for me. This was limited to kids that were around 8-10 years old. They were old enough to understand the rules of the game while just being old enough to try to learn some of the basic skills involved with the sport. Some were there because their parents made them, but for the most part, they enjoyed the game and wanted to improve and have fun.

With my mom being an elementary school teacher, I'd been around lots of kids in my wheelchair, so I wasn't too nervous about their reactions; I knew how to handle and ease any fears or answer any questions they may have had. I was truly more scared as to how the parents would react to their kids having a coach that was in a wheelchair. Luckily, I never had a problem with any parents who had doubts or concerns. I give them a lot of credit for allowing me to prove myself, but I also think my actions proved there was no need for them to be concerned.

Unfortunately, my coaching record didn't get off to too much of a better start than my playing days. I know we won more than one game that first season, but we were at the bottom of the standings. As a first-year coach, I was given all first-year players. There's a huge difference in the physical maturity and development of an eight-year-old boy compared to a ten-year-old boy. The first half of the season was devoted to just getting my team to stay in the batter's box during live pitching. My philosophy was to rotate everybody around in the field so they could gain experience at all the positions. There were a few exceptions because not everybody was suited to play first base, pitch, or be the catcher.

Finding players to be our catcher was always an adventure. There was one boy I could always count on, but catching a full game was just too difficult for somebody that size and age. The league had a rule: *All catchers have to wear a cup in order to be behind the plate.* Trying to explain this rule to the team at the beginning of the season was not the easiest thing to do. First of all, for more than half of the players, the only cup they had ever known was something to drink out of. I can just imagine what they were picturing in their heads as I was trying to tactfully describe what an athletic cup is, where it goes, and why one must be worn by catchers. For many games, our catcher was determined simply by who happened to be wearing a cup that day. There were a couple of times when I'd have a player tell me he was wearing a cup and wanted to try out catching. Let me tell you that with eight-year-old boys, the eye doesn't lie when it comes to telling whether or not a boy is wearing his cup!

There was also the case of one mom complaining to me after a game because her son had never played first base. In the kindest way possible I had to explain to her that it was for her son's own safety. I hate saying it, but this kid couldn't have caught a ball even if it was dropped into his mitt. My fear was having him at first base and getting drilled in the face, or some other vital body part, by a throw from one of my other players. She wasn't thrilled with my explanation, but the bottom line was he never played first base.

Even though we didn't have the greatest record, we definitely improved as the season went on. There was a game-saving catch in the outfield just like you'd see in the movies: eyes closed, head turned the other way, glove raised in the air and the ball somehow finding a way directly into the mitt . . . and staying there. We also executed a perfect relay, outfielder to shortstop to catcher, to tag out a base runner attempting to score off a hit. The look on my catcher's face as the umpire called the runner out was priceless. It was as if by tagging one runner out at home plate, he all of a sudden could envision himself playing in the big leagues.

I guess the league liked how I handled and coached the younger kids, because the next summer they asked me to coach another new team with boys just entering the league. My team from the previous summer ended up being coached by a couple of their dads. It was tough seeing how they physically matured and were using lots of the techniques I had taught them. It would have been nice to continue to be a part of their development, but I wasn't about to complain. Once again, it was back to the very basics. I knew with the team being so young, if the players didn't have a positive experience they might just ditch the sport and decide not to participate in upcoming seasons. I tried not to put pressure on myself in that way, but I knew if all else failed, I could always win them over with the post-game treat! We finished towards the bottom of the standings, but overall we played well considering most of my boys were so skinny they could fit inside the team equipment bag while other teams primarily had boys carrying their own bat bags.

I ended up coaching for two more summers before I had to hang-up the clipboard due to an internship and eventually a job. I know I taught my teams a lot about the game of baseball, but I also can say I taught them some things about the game of life. They may never remember "Coach Mo" by name, but they will always remember the coach they had who was in a wheelchair. It won't be because of something I couldn't do or something specific I did differently, but rather for being a regular coach who just happened to be in a wheelchair. That's exactly how I had hoped they'd perceive me. For the majority, I'm sure I was the first person in a wheelchair with whom they had ever really had any interaction. Hopefully, being around me broke any preconceived ideas they had towards others with physical disabilities. I hope every one of my players has had a moment since then when they could have negatively stereotyped another individual, but instead remembered being a part of that baseball team, and kept an open mind due to our relationship. At the same time, I credit those kids for giving me so much of the confidence I have today. Had my coaching experience turned out to be a negative one, I'm not sure I would have taken on so many of the titles, activities, and challenges I have later on in life.

Even though I was still finding ways for sports to remain a part of my life by keeping score, officiating and coaching, it just wasn't the same as actually competing and having an impact on the final score. For somebody as competitive as I was—and still am—not being able to physically participate left a huge void in my life. Both physically and mentally, I needed to have a release, and it wasn't available . . . yet.

CHAPTER 4

66 **Y**OU ONLY get one best friend in life, and you're mine." I'll never forget those words spoken to me by Kevin Sonnemann. It was after Mandy and I had broken up, my girlfriend of more than three years. I realized I had neglected my friendship with Kevin and was wondering why he had never complained or wasn't holding anything against me. Not many people would have put up with going from first chair to second fiddle and then accepted the friend back at number one. That's just one more example of how lucky I am to have Kevin as my best friend.

At less than a year of age, our friendship began. With his mom as my daycare provider, it's a good thing we got along, or else it would have made for an awful start to both of our lives. We did everything together and wanted to spend every minute together. It wasn't enough that we were together all day Monday through Friday; on the weekends we'd make one of our parents take us to the other's house to play. I always preferred going over to Kevin's house as I felt he had the better toys, but he made his fair share of trips over to my house. We didn't live too far away from each other, but we were basically just out of walking distance. It would have made things a lot easier had we been able to walk to each other's house, but we didn't see any inconvenience in asking for transportation each way.

We liked all of the same types of games, especially board games. The only problem was that the rules we learned from our own families didn't always match up. The main objective of each game would be the same, but there would always seem to be one rule here or there that would be slightly different.

Kevin and I have always had different personalities, as far as how vocal or social we are. Kevin is much more quiet, bordering on being shy, while I am much more vocal and don't mind being in front of large audiences. One characteristic we both do share is we're both very competitive and hate losing. This ended up causing some problems when deciding who was right or wrong as far as rules were concerned. We ended up having two ways to play various games, one with "Kevin's Rules" and the other with "Mo's Rules", depending on whose house we happened to be playing at. For some reason, when playing at Kevin's, I was always accused of cheating, particularly when we'd play Parcheesi. More than with any other game, that one irritated me the most. My grandmother who lived in Baltimore taught my brother and me how to play, and we'd play for hours upon hours with her. She taught me every single rule of that game, and now I was being told I wasn't playing right. By saying I wasn't playing right, it was like Kevin was saying my grandmother didn't know how to play the game. Everybody knows grandmothers know all the rules inside and out when it comes to games. It's just part of the initiation process or something they all have to go through in order to be certified. To this day, Kevin's mom still teases me about having to play by "Mo's Rules". I don't see what the problem is; after all, it's just the right way to play the game!

Even though we spent countless hours playing various board games, sports were still both of our passions. Along with my dad coaching baseball and other sports, Kevin's dad was the high school assistant wrestling coach and eventually the school's athletic director. Since Kevin was wrestling,

I too wrestled for a brief period growing up. I still have the ribbons I received as a participant in the city-wide tournament held each year. Obviously in a sport where strength is such a key component, I had to rely heavily on technique. I guess my technique wasn't all that great either, because I got pinned more than my fair share. My greatest achievement was actually advancing to face Kevin in a match and taking him the full length without getting pinned, the first time I had been able to do that in a competitive match.

Nerf basketball was another constant in our friendship. Whether it was one-on-one or games of H-O-R-S-E, we spent hours with that little foam ball in our hands and a plastic rim hooked over the top of a door. I have no idea how many extra balls we ended up purchasing over the years as they all seemed to get chunks taken out of them at various times or would just disappear out of the blue. The rim must have had a full roll of masking tape on it after snapping in different places due to our attempts at being Michael Jordan or Dominique Wilkins with our dunks; I should really say Kevin's attempts. Jumping never really was one of my assets. I preferred the Larry Bird or Bill Laimbeer school of thought where jumping high enough to just clear a piece of paper was enough.

The kitchen in Kevin's house had a countertop or island in the middle of it with a walk-in storage closet on one side where we placed the rim on top of its entrance door. If we made a shot from behind the island, it was considered a three pointer. I knew I would never be able to beat Kevin by faking him out or taking shots with him guarding me closer to the basket; he constantly had an extra few inches on me growing up. Goal tending wasn't something we concerned ourselves with other than saying you couldn't blatantly stick your hand through the bottom of the rim and swat a shot away that was already going through the basket. If one person made a basket, the other had to take the ball back behind the other side of the island before being allowed to take a shot. We also decided the defender had to take the ball back to the other side of the island in a clockwise rotation, along with the person who took the shot having to do the same, so no one could try to set a pick and slow down the other person's attempt to change over to offense. My whole game was based on two different shots. If I got back behind the island, or our three-point line, before Kevin was able to station himself under the basket, I would attempt a three-pointer. If he was able to get under the basket before I took that shot, I would try to post him up with my back to the basket and do my best Robert Parish impression. I was a Celtics fan growing up, so it was never the Kareem Abdul-Jabbar skyhook. I actually became quite good at the hook-shot and probably gave Kevin more letters while playing HORSE with that shot compared to any other. I'm still a little amazed to this day why more post players don't develop that shot. If it worked for the NBA's all-time leading scorer, you'd think others would take note. I guess it isn't a Sports Center highlight, so players don't practice it anymore; go figure.

We'd set the timer on the microwave and actually play regulation-length four quarter games. Between quarters we'd take water breaks and think over our sophisticated Nerf basketball game plans. Any cooking in the kitchen that needed to be done would have to take a back seat to one of our games. I was always sort of amazed I could hold my own against Kevin. This was a guy that ended up playing varsity basketball through his senior year in high school, and I competed with him growing up with a severe disadvantage physically.

It wasn't until a random conversation I was having with my dad and somebody else a few years back, that my dad casually said something to the effect that perhaps Kevin hadn't been playing at his best, just so I could keep things close. My dad wasn't trying to be derogatory, and it came up only because he was trying to explain to the other person how special our relationship has been. It was like seeing something for the first time only to realize it had been there all along. I'm still not sure if it is even true; maybe that's just me being a little naïve; nevertheless, if it is true, to this day Kevin has never said one thing or given any impression he was letting me keep the games close. I've never known a person with a smaller ego or personal agenda. I'm sure if I asked Kevin, he'd say he wasn't letting me keep the score close or even win every now and then. That's okay, there are times you're better off not knowing the whole truth. For me, they're memories that put a smile on my face and will for the remainder of my life; I know they do the same for Kevin.

Ping pong—now there's a sport I could hold my own in. There's no running around, no jumping, not a whole bunch of muscle or strength needed—just good hand-eye coordination, accuracy, and a little trickery now and then. For Christmas one year, my parents got my brother and me a ping-pong table. I had to be in either the fourth or fifth grade because it was close to when we had just moved in to our new house located at 726 Alcona Court—our new house that could also be labeled as our new, "more muscular dystrophy friendly" house. It was a ranch style where you entered on the main level where my bedroom was also located. Our previous house had three floors to it and required going up a few steps just to get inside. It was not a good place for a child with mobility issues to be growing up in.

When it comes to ping pong, if Kevin were to tell you he let me keep those scores close and allowed me to win some games, I'd say he was lying. As far as my memories go, I actually held a slight advantage in our win/loss record against each other. He'd probably tell you otherwise, but that's just our competitive juices flowing.

If our basketball games lasted a long time, then our ping pong matches were like marathons. We would play actually using a tennis-match scoring system. Individual games were played with standard ping-pong rules to 21, having to win by two points; but matches consisted of the best of five sets with a set concluding with the first person to win 6 games or through a tie-breaker system like is done in tennis. As you can imagine, this would take a very long time to complete, sometimes lasting over the period of a couple of days during the summer or weekends during the school year. We'd end up having to post the scores on a piece of paper so there wouldn't be any discrepancy should we have to stop a contest between games until another day.

Ping pong was also the source of the only fight Kevin and I ever got into with each other. To this day, we each have our own variation of the story that caused the only black eye in our relationship, at least figuratively. Trust me, there have also been many black eyes, literally, but those were just from having fun and boys being boys, not from us fighting.

During the summer, Kevin's parents ran a camp in southern Michigan that was designed for people with emotional, cognitive, or other developmental disabilities. I'd always go down for a week and play with Kevin, not as a camper, but just as a friend. Our room was located upstairs in the main building or lodge, and in the lobby was a ping-pong table, a perfect stage to hold our five-set competitions.

Kevin and I were in the midst of one of our epic ping-pong battles when the dinner bell rang. We went and ate, and as soon as we were done, we rushed back to the lobby to continue our contest. That's when things turned ugly, at least as far as our words were concerned.

We both have our own versions of what took place from there, down to the very finest detail; but one thing is for sure, to this day we still disagree on the score. We get a good laugh about it when we tell people nowadays, but at the time we were truly mad at each other. It wasn't even a specific play or ruling we disagreed on; it was simply the score to resume our match. Looking back on it, I truly believe both of us thought we were correct. I don't think one was trying to cheat the other or get an upper hand. The only way both of us would get that mad was if we both thought the other was lying. No punches were thrown, but there was some slamming of the paddles, throwing balls, and lots of yelling.

We of course were punished for our disturbance and weren't allowed to play for the remainder of the night or do any other activities together. Luckily, as is the case with most boys, we woke up the next morning as if nothing had happened and started a brand new match. That's not to say we forgot about the previous night's event, we just chose to move forward. After all, there was still a ping-pong table in the lobby calling our names! Over thirty years together as best friends and only one fight—if you can even call that a fight—is not a bad track record. I could write story after story of adventures we had growing up or give endless examples of the strength of our friendship, but one story is still ongoing and tells it all.

As a young kid, I'm sure Kevin realized I was slower than others, but I never once recall it coming up in any conversation. After being diagnosed, my parents knew in the simplest terms something had to be said to Kevin to explain what would be happening to me. Sometimes the easiest explanations are done by using the simplest terms. Luckily, the Muscular Dystrophy Association produces a publication specifically targeted for young children who are friends of somebody just diagnosed with a form of muscular dystrophy. My parents gave the pamphlet to Kevin's mom who then read it to Kevin.

Not knowing how Kevin would react to hearing his best friend was different than others and would be getting weaker as the two of us grew up together, she asked Kevin if he had any questions or wanted to talk about anything. Without any hesitation, Kevin looked back at his mom and made one statement, "I want to cure muscular dystrophy."

Right then Kevin knew what he wanted to do when he grew up. While most boys say they want to be fire fighters, professional athletes or astronauts, Kevin had a new vision. He wanted to grow up and find a cure for his best friend. It's one thing for an eight-year-old boy to make that statement; it's another for a thirty-year-old man to be following through on that promise.

After graduating from college with a B.S. in Biology and Chemistry, Kevin went on and obtained his Ph.D. in Cellular and Molecular Biology. He is currently a Research Associate in the Department of Biochemistry, Molecular Biology, and Biophysics at the University of Minnesota and has had his research published in multiple publications. He's traveled the world, giving presentations and discussing his research.

If you ask Kevin, he'll tell you his desire is to someday be a high school teacher and coach. The problem is that Kevin is a man of his word, and he made the promise that he'd find a cure for his best friend in life. Don't get me wrong; you couldn't find somebody more passionate about his work. It's just that the passion comes from something only the two of us could feel or explain.

You only get one best friend in life, and he's mine.

CHAPTER 5

You don't get to pick who your parents are in life, and for this I'm thankful—reason being that there's no way I could have picked two better ones than what I'm blessed to have.

I was once asked, "If I had the chance to start my life all over again with the guarantee I would be born without a form of muscular dystrophy and be completely healthy, but risk having different parents, would I take it?" The answer is "no," and I don't have to take an extra second to think it over.

The biggest compliment I can give to my parents is from day-one of my diagnosis, they HAVE treated me differently than they treated my older brother. At first this may sound counter intuitive. Shouldn't parents treat all their kids the same? The truth of the matter is that a child with a disability is different, but there is nothing wrong with that. The sooner a family can accept the differences, the sooner it can move forward and realize how much is still the same. Expectations and dreams should still be high; it just may take a different route to realize them. It's also fairly common for parents to turn against each other when they have a child with a disability. Luckily, this didn't happen to mine. If anything, it strengthened their relationship and brought our family closer together.

My parents enjoy many of the same things in life, but they are very different from each other. In many ways, that's what makes them such a wonderful couple. My mom is quick on her feet when it comes to making decisions during stressful or emergency situations. Ask her to pick out a package of cookies at the grocery store, and we'll be standing in the aisle long enough for the milk to go bad in our shopping cart. She could spend a whole day sitting on a park bench just watching various people go about their business and be as happy as a dog with a new squeaky toy. My mom also has a tendency to say whatever is on her mind and, as a result, can either stick her foot in her mouth or appear as if she is competing with Yogi Berra for the latest "Yogi-ism".

I remember one summer, my girlfriend and I were getting ready to go watch the National Cherry Festival Parade, which takes place every summer the week after the 4th of July and is huge in my hometown of Traverse City. My mom started talking about her favorite floats which appeared in the parade year after year and then decided she would mention one float that was her least favorite and hoped wouldn't appear again. Of course, it just happened to be the one float my girlfriend appeared on as a little girl growing up. My mom had no way of knowing this, but it didn't shock me at all that she happened to pick the one.

My mom is also the same person that when she was describing my brother's girlfriend, Jinny, for the first time to some of her friends, she described her as The All-American Girl. This typically would paint the picture of somebody with blonde hair and blue eyes. The problem is that Jinny is Korean and was adopted as a baby by her parents in the United States—not exactly what I would call The All-American Girl!

My mom also thought it was a little strange that a radio station would be a sponsor for the walk-in urgent-care facility that recently opened up in town. It wasn't until after I reminded her that normal body temperature is 98.6 degrees that she realized the new 98.6 After Hours Urgent Care facility was in reference to good health and not a music station.

Not to go overboard and tease my mom too much, but I have to get in one more example. Down the road from my parents' house is a video rental store. Outside the entrance, there is naturally a large sign advertising the store with its name. Now in order for this story to be funny, you have to remember we live in East Lansing. The name of the store was E.L. Video—simple enough. Well, one night my mom suggested we rent a video over the weekend, so I recommended she get a membership at the video rental store down the road. She sort of looked back at me with a confused expression and then asked why she would want to rent Spanish videos. For the life of me, I couldn't figure out what she was talking about, and then it dawned on me. She thought E.L. Video was really *El Video* as in the Spanish translation of The Video. I love my mom!

As an elementary teacher in the Traverse City public school system for over thirty years, my mom was amazing at what she was able to provide to her students—or better stated, her *children*—as she took a personal interest in each and every one of them. Now retired, I can tell she still misses being in the classroom and teaching. She was a natural at what she did and had a passion and love for her job. If it weren't for the politics, parents, and sometimes lack of community respect for the profession, I believe she would still be teaching today.

My dad also was employed in the public school system, teaching exactly half of his career at the high-school level and the other half junior high. He is one of those classic examples of being a child that was constantly into all kinds of mischief, finding his way into trouble and that wound up in the profession he had least likely seen in his future . . . back in the classroom as a teacher. My dad was one of those teachers that when you were going through his class, you dreaded it because of the high expectations and amount of work he demanded. After you were through and looked back on the experience, you knew you were better because of it.

I think part of the reason he was such a good teacher was because, in his own way, he was able to relate to the students. He may not have had the greatest fashion sense, nor did he know any of the latest Hollywood stars, but he was able to capture the students that other teachers might have ignored. After all, this was the same guy that as a boy made a phone call into the Baltimore public school system to cancel school due to a snow storm and the same boy who had his mom convinced he had been promoted and allowed to skip a grade in school only to have her show up at the school to complete the proper paper work and have the principal look at her with an expression mixed between confusion and amusement.

As a married couple, they make the perfect team. Growing up I never recall what could be termed as a fight between the two of them. Sure there were arguments here and there, but never a full-blown-out fight. My mom teases me that I get all nervous or bent out of shape when I see the two of them argue. As a joke, she says she should really get into an all-out shouting match with my dad, so I can see what the majority of marriages these days look like. I simply tease her back by saying, "I should yell at the top of my lungs back at you, so you can know what the relationship between lots of parents and their children look like!" We both know we are lucky with how close we are with each other.

My dad is the more emotional one between my parents. I don't know if that was always the case, but after my diagnosis, there was no doubt about it. He's not wimpy or what could be termed as overly feminine, but he loves his family more than anything in the whole entire world and cries very easily. It's his way of dealing with stress; and if he wasn't able to release his emotions, I'm sure it would be awful for his physical health.

I can't think of a more even-keeled person than my dad, but he's not very cognizant of his surroundings. A new store could go in on a street corner that he'd pass every day, and it might be six months later until he sees it and announces a new store has gone in. His heart is always in the right place, but he'll make silly mistakes. For example, my mom will frequently get up early in the mornings to go for walks. Oftentimes she would drive over to my apartment and pick up my service dog Ted, and take him along for some added exercise. One morning my dad was awakened by some thunder, and seeing my mom wasn't in bed next to him, he assumed she was caught out walking in the storm. He threw on some clothes and hurried out of the house as quickly as possible, got in his car, and went out to find my mom to pick her up.

Mom, not being an idiot, hadn't gotten up early to go walking in the storm, but was awakened by the thunder, couldn't get back to sleep, and was watching the morning news in their sun porch, which is located basically right next to the door leading into their bedroom. While enjoying her morning coffee, all of a sudden she saw my dad make a mad dash out of their bedroom and head out the front door. She assumed he was going to grab the morning paper, but couldn't quite figure out what the huge rush was all about. After a few minutes had passed and my dad still hadn't returned back inside, my mom got a little concerned. She went to look out the front window and noticed the car was gone. In this day and age, the simple thing would normally have been to call my dad on his cell phone and figure out what was going on. However, my dad doesn't believe in carrying cell phones even though he has one. I know, it doesn't make sense to me either, but I'm beyond the point of trying to figure it out. Don't ask him why he also didn't try calling my mom on her phone before assuming she was stuck or even to find out her specific location. He just doesn't think these types of things through. Anyway, my mom figured it would only make things worse to get in the other car to go find him, so she did the only thing she could: wait for him to return back home. Finally, about an hour later, my dad returned back at the house and entered the front door with his gear all wet and a look on his face crossed between scared, confused, and upset. Seeing the pitiful expression, my mom put all the pieces together and just started laughing. After explaining she just thought he was going outside to get the morning paper, which is why she didn't say anything to stop him, my dad did the only thing he could at that point. He went and took a hot shower! Bottom line: what's right under his nose, or blatantly obvious to others, doesn't always strike a chord with my dad.

Nobody ever really wants to make another person cry, and I believe that's the reason I usually don't go to my dad first when I'm dealing with an emotional issue. I'm talking about my normal everyday situations or difficulties that arise. On the other hand, I can't think of another person I would rather have with me than my dad when dealing with true emergency situations. He was a medic while serving in the United States Air Force, and that training and experience still remains in him. He has an unbelievable ability to remain calm under pressure and keep a level head. I've never once seen my dad lose his cool. He has a quiet self-confidence that can't be knocked, the same quality he received from his dad and passed down through my brother.

My mom, on the other hand, is just like a best friend at times for me. I share everything with her—well, almost everything! If families have a rock that holds everything together, she's ours. She has the ability to listen to my problems and help me sort out my thoughts. It's very difficult for parents of a child with a disability to know what to say or think since they have never experienced the same physical differences or weaknesses. She has never tried to assume she knows what I'm going through or experiencing, but has a special way of trying to put herself in my situation and help me through whatever I may be struggling with at that moment. Ultimately, the choice has to be mine, and she does everything within her power to let me know she'll support and honor whatever choices I make.

I know it hurts my dad sometimes that I always go to my mom first when I'm struggling with something. It's not that I don't trust my dad or that I don't feel close to him, it's just I think it is normal for children to naturally gravitate towards one parent or the other. For me it happens to be my mom.

I'm the first person to admit I am very short fussed when it comes to dealing with my parents. Not that it makes it right, but most people are this way with the people they love the most. Maybe it's because we take them for granted or assume they'll always be there, but I know I would never treat or say some of the things to other people I say to my parents. I get frustrated quite easily. I require a lot of assistance with some of the easiest tasks in life, and routine is very important in making sure those tasks get performed in the most efficient way possible.

For example, putting my shoes and socks on before putting on a shirt that goes over my head is important because that way I can put my feet on the footrests of my wheelchair to gain the extra trunk balance I need. You'd think after all these years my parents would remember this without having to think twice. Well, that's not always the case and this just infuriates me. For some reason I can't just calmly say, "Please help me with my shoes and socks first." I have to shake my head or swing my foot until it dawns on them that I'm not going to cooperate until they go in the right order. I'm constantly trying to work on this aspect of my temperament, but at the same time, that stubbornness has helped me get to where I currently am professionally in my life.

I do have to say that it's not always my fault when a conflict arises between my parents and me. It's always tough in its own right for parents to let go of their children and allow them to make their own decisions in life and become an adult. This is only compounded with the dynamics of the relationship when a disability is thrown into the equation.

I seem to think my parents frequently forget I'm thirty years old. I say this because even though I am thirty, I require some of the same assistance that a five-year-old requires. Neither I nor a five-year-old is in diapers; we're both fine once we're up in the morning, but we need assistance getting dressed. Both are able to fix snacks or zap things in the microwave, but using the stove really isn't the safest option. They want to be a part of my life so badly and make sure I have everything I need to be as independent as possible that they can tend to swarm me so much to the extent it's impossible for me to be independent. I appreciate everything they do for me more than the world, but sometimes I have to ask them to think about what their lives were like and what they were doing when *they* were in their thirties. It's a cruel paradox because as much as I want my independence from them, I want and need their assistance. Luckily I have two parents that realize this and do everything within their power to be the best parents I could ever ask for.

CHAPTER 6

I DON'T REALLY recall going through the stage most boys do when girls become the enemy or have cooties. While I was never mistaken as the class flirt, my testosterone levels were present at an early age. This made things quite difficult for me as I became cognizant of looks and body image early on. Due to my previous prednisone fiasco and dosage, as a young boy I knew I was overweight for my age and I walked differently than everybody else, but there was nothing I could do about it. I had to come to the early realization that I would never be able to win a girl over by being a jock or having the physique of a male model. Of course the dating life of a boy in his pre-teens isn't very complex.

My brother was the opposite when it came to girls. He wasn't interested in them at all growing up and would much rather prefer to be playing ball or some other activity than ask a girl out on a date. I struggled with this as I wanted to ask my big brother questions about girls and dating, but figured there was no point as I estimated I had just as much as experience as he did—none. In some ways I felt guilty about liking girls. There was nothing dirty about it or anything like that, it was just in my head that I felt my brother was supposed to have a girlfriend, or at least be going out on dates, before I did. You've heard of reverse psychology; well, this was reverse pressure, the pressure to actually *not* do something.

My core group of friends also lagged behind me when it came to puberty and having eyes for the opposite sex. Although this did nothing to lessen the desires of a boy who was starting to understand that the birds and the bees was more than just a catchy song lyric, it would have made things a lot worse had there been the added pressure of seeing and hearing about my friends dating experiences. None of them really ever wanted to go to dances being put on by our school or local churches. I, on the other hand, very badly wanted to go, but was way too intimidated to actually ask a girl. It's tough enough for a boy to overcome his natural fears of asking a girl out, but I had extenuating circumstances. What if I lost my balance while dancing and fell in front of everybody. Of course I would be embarrassed, but what about the girl I was dancing with? Wouldn't she feel humiliated, and would there ever be another girl that would risk dancing with me in public? On top of that, if for some miracle things went well, that meant I would have to actually come up with other dates to go out on. I was trying to avoid that situation for some strange twisted reasoning that seemed logical in my messed-up head.

As a young child, I always enjoyed dancing with my mom. I have great memories of being in our kitchen with the radio playing and doing twirls and dips with her. I don't really know where my sense of rhythm and musical abilities come from. There isn't much inherited rhythm on either side of my family. Actually, I'm being nice by just saying there isn't "much"; in actuality, there is none. I have trouble just trying to keep my dad on beat as he's clapping to the MSU Fight Song.

My first non-Mom dance experience came while I was in the seventh grade. My church youth group was the sponsor for the event and it, along with other dating firsts, is something I will always remember in full detail. I got there early, as I was part of the set-up crew. My church was shaped somewhat like a "U", and to get from one end to the other, you either stay inside and walk through the whole building or go outside and cross on the sidewalk to get to the other entrance. I needed to get to the other side to bring some decorations back to the area where the dance was going to take place, so I decided to take the shortcut by myself and go outside. Being that it was winter in northern Michigan, the sidewalk was slippery, and I was in a hurry to get out of the cold—not a good combination for somebody who is shaky on his feet. Needless to say, down I went. Luckily I didn't seriously hurt anything, and somehow I was able to get myself back up, but the condition of my pants was another story. The sidewalk had just been salted, so the snow and ice had turned to that partially liquid state, which my pants soaked up instantly. Here I was at my first dance, and my pants looked as if I had some kind of weird backwards bathroom accident. I knew I couldn't go back to where the dance was being set up as everybody would want to know what happened. If I actually told them the truth, they'd be concerned about my physical condition first, and then in an attempt to make me feel better, say the state of my pants wasn't all that noticeable. Come on people . . . we're talking about seventh and eighth graders here; that's the same age group that can tell you what anybody wore from head to toe three weeks ago and if they've worn any of those same clothes since that day. Image is everything!

Luckily, I knew the layout of the church, so I continued outside and entered the opposite doors. There was a set of bathrooms on that end, and I knew the men's room was equipped with an electric hot-air hand dryer. It was mounted a little high for my plan, but certainly was my best option. After multiple restarts and a butt that was scorching hot—and I'm not talking in the sexy kind of way—I made my way back, albeit the long way inside, to the dance. My pants were a little dirty, but it was hardly noticeable with how dark the room was.

Any confidence I had built up that day for the dance had been eliminated in the blink of an eye. My nightmare of falling had become a reality; luckily it just hadn't happened in front of everybody. There was no way, no matter how badly I wanted to, was I going to ask a girl to dance. I spent the majority of the rest of the night holding up a wall with all the other guys who were too embarrassed to ask a girl to dance and the remaining girls that hadn't been asked—not exactly the group of people you want to be hanging out with on a regular basis.

But a funny thing happened before the night was over. Instead of being one of the worst nights of my childhood, it turned out to be one of the greatest. It's amazing how a single event can turn everything around. I was never able to work up the confidence to ask somebody to dance, but the act of one girl, Meredith, changed my night. I'll never forget her, as she actually asked me if I wanted to dance.

Did I want to dance with her? Let's see, she had known me for a few years, so she knew she was asking somebody who had a physical disability. Not only was she not ugly, but she was good looking and let's just say she was well past the training-bra stage, something all seventh grade boys notice! This wasn't an image breaker; this was an image builder. YES, I wanted to dance with her. The song I can't remember, but it didn't last nearly long enough. I had just turned thirteen a few months previously, so it's not like I was Patrick Swayze in *Dirty Dancing*. I was more like Kevin Arnold dancing with Winnie Cooper in *The Wonder Years*. Just picture hands straight out, rocking side to side. This was my first true dance with a girl, and the feel of her hips on my hands was amazing. I don't think I actually danced to any other song the remainder of the night, but that didn't matter. With one dance, I was officially promoted from a child to a teenager. I wouldn't frequent too many other dances growing up, but with the act of one girl asking me for a single dance, I realized my dating life wouldn't have to be a complete void due to my disability.

The next couple of years were mostly uneventful as far as my dating experiences were concerned. I was still following the pretense that my brother was supposed to have a girlfriend before I jumped into anything. Unfortunately, he still hadn't been bitten by the dating bug, and it certainly wasn't due to girls not liking him. Had I been in his shoes, it would have been a totally different story. I think his non-interest in girls actually made some of them flirt or attempt to get him to notice them even more. Here I was not asking girls out because I didn't want to violate some brotherly rite of passage I had mysteriously created on my own, and he was turning girls down!

As a high school freshman, however, I finally just said enough was enough. I realized I needed to sew some oats of my own. In my hometown of Traverse City, the junior high was seventh through the ninth grade, so I was still at a different building than my brother, who was entering his senior year of high school. I couldn't use him as an excuse anymore. Even though my intentions were good, I think subconsciously I was using him as an excuse to cover up my intense fear of rejection. I needed to take another step forward in my teenage passage.

A simple smile or little feminine wave can send a boy absolutely soaring, or at least it could with me. My hormones were raging, and I was determined to do something about it. I've always been good at flirting; it's just getting beyond the flirt and actually asking a girl out where I've struggled. If I have one regret growing up, it's I didn't ask more girls out. I'm not saying I needed to be with a different girl every other week, or have a new flavor of the month, but just to have had more dating experiences would have been nice.

I definitely had more than my fair share of crushes, although I never had the crush on a teacher most boys experience. I could sit here and fill a whole page with the names of girls that caught my eye, but there was one, more than any other, that totally put me in a daze and would continue to do so until she moved away. To this day, the thoughts of Laura Fajardo can still mesmerize me. She had it all: very popular, athletic, funny, extremely good looking, and to put the cherry on the top, she was even smart! She was the type of girl you'd figure was out of the league of all the guys her own age and was probably dating an older guy in high school. Yet for some strange reason, I always felt as if there was a slim chance she might actually consider going out with me.

I had noticed her as both a seventh and eighth grader—I mean how could you miss her, but in the ninth grade our schedules somewhat matched because we had a couple of classes together. As I got to know Laura by being with her daily in class, my feelings just intensified. I was amazed at how intelligent she was, and she didn't try to come across as some ditzy bombshell so many girls were trying to portray. We had a civics class with one of my favorite teachers, Mr. Bauer. He was the type of teacher that really made students think about their beliefs and how those beliefs impacted not only themselves, but others around them. He wasn't afraid to bring up controversial issues and discuss hot topics that were in the media at the time. Without fail, Laura and I always seemed to be on the same page and voice our opinions together. In my head, it was as if we were made for each other. Unfortunately, I never worked up the confidence to do anything about it.

I really don't know if I believe in fate, but I do believe God has a way of putting us in certain places at certain times that can't be explained any other way than to simply say that He's looking over us. The summer following my sophomore year, I was just becoming comfortable enough with using a power wheelchair to go out and be seen in public. I was still able to walk, but I would fatigue fairly quickly and wasn't very stable on my feet. One new door it opened was the ability to go for "walks" with my mom, as she had previously just been going on her own or with our family dog around our neighborhood. As luck, or fate, or destiny would have it, one day as we were out together and approaching our neighborhood, I noticed a jogger coming toward us from the opposite direction. As she was getting closer and closer, my hormones were telling me that this was somebody worth checking out. Boy, was that the understatement of the year. It turned out to be Laura, and being that I was in my wheelchair, she recognized me well before she would have passed us. As she got closer, it seemed as if she was actually slowing down and was going to stop, or at least pause, to say hi.

Could I have been more embarrassed than to be seen with my mom and in my wheelchair? Here was Laura, out jogging on her own, and I was with my "mommy". It's amazing how embarrassing it is to be seen with one or your parents when you're a teenager; it's almost comical when you look back on it.

My mom must have seen my eyes dancing and heard my voice quiver when I said "Hi, Laura," because without hesitation she told me to take my time and she'd meet me back at our house. I doubt my mom has the slightest recollection of that day, but it will forever be engraved in my head for two reasons. First, my mom did one of her best parenting jobs that day. It would have been so easy for her to just stay there with me or stand to the side and wait for me to finish talking with Laura. She realized I was growing up and needed some space in this situation. She recognized the importance of it all as I was out in my wheelchair and here was an attractive girl that stopped on her own to talk with me. She knew how important it was for me to experience the same emotions other boys my age felt and gain the additional confidence I would need throughout the remainder of my adolescence. Second, this was Laura Fajardo we're talking about here; of course it is going to be engraved in my head!

I knew Laura was moving sometime that summer, so I figured this was probably the last time I'd see her, yet alone talk with her. I'm sure she could tell I was flustered as we were talking, but she probably was used to that, as it can be intimidating for guys to talk to girls who they are so attracted to. I had so many thoughts rushing through my head. *Should I tell her how I'd always felt about her, or should I just let her lead the conversation and go with it wherever she took it?* It didn't matter to me as long as I could keep the conversation going for as long as possible. Before saying good-bye, I found out she was actually moving away in just a couple of days. I didn't profess my feelings or come up with some grand love poem; I'm not even sure if I said I'd miss her. There was no Disney or fairytale ending as I didn't get a farewell kiss or hug. Even so, that was an important day in my adolescence, and I know God put both of us in that spot on that day for a reason. For whatever her reasons, Laura decided to stop and talk with me, as opposed to just waving and saying hi in passing as she jogged by, which I will always appreciate. We had never bumped into each other at any other time outside of school before that day; but there we were, just the two of us, having our own little date, as far-fetched as that may be.

Laura ended up moving out of state before our junior year, to New Jersey if I remember correctly. I never asked her out, but she'll always be that one girl that will linger in the back of my head and raise the question, "What if . . . ?"

My first official girlfriend was Rebecca (Becca) Ligon. We basically hung around the same group of friends, most of whom were dating each other, so the time had come for me to step up to the plate. The flirting sort of hit a climax at a birthday party; I was at the top of my game. Being the mature 15-year-old I was, the following day I had to ask one of our mutual friends if she thought Becca would actually "go out" with me. She felt fairly confident the answer would be yes, so all that was left was for me to ask. I don't recall if I did it that day or waited until the next, but I finally asked Becca if she wanted to be my girlfriend. Once again, I'm so thankful her answer was "Yes", because had I been rejected, I don't know how long it would have taken me to recover and ask out another girl.

I couldn't tell you how long the two of us went out together. I know we hit at least the two-month mark, but it didn't last much longer than that. We handed our fair share of notes to each other while passing in the hallways and went to some movies with our group of friends, but really didn't do a whole bunch as just the two of us. We were both too young to have a driver's license, so doing anything that didn't involve being with a group was more complicated because more than likely it meant getting a ride from our parents—just the people a teenage couple don't want to include on their date. Getting any kind of privacy was a huge challenge.

As guys tend to do, they push and pry to see how much action their other guy friends are getting. It's quite easy for stories to get embellished, and I'm sure half of the stuff mentioned never even comes close to occurring. Anyway, I had been dating Becca for a while and was getting asked by my friends for any and all details concerning our love life. Now let's also put this in perspective. I was just in the ninth grade, this was my first girlfriend, and when it came to my friends' sexual exploits, they were about as racy as a G-movie. It's not like I would have had to come up with a story of being alone in my room with her and my parents being out of the house. A simple line about making out in the darkness of a movie theater would have been just fine. But for some reason I couldn't even do that, so I briefly had to put up with my friends teasing me about not getting any action.

I guess Becca was dealing with the same thing, because a few days later all of a sudden I became "The Man". No, the two of us didn't do anything that couldn't be mentioned in these pages, and we didn't hold our own make-out session in a supply closet at school. As a matter of fact, we didn't do anything! My understanding of the whole situation is one day while riding home on the bus, Becca must have told some of my friends we had our first kiss together, and it must have been more than just a peck on the cheek or lips because I got all kinds of hand slaps and pats on the back the following day. It took me a minute to piece everything together, but I certainly didn't deny any of it and was quite proud of my newfound manhood. It might be the first case of locker room talk being initiated by the girl, but either way it took a lot of pressure off me.

The truth be told, the whole time the two of us dated, we never once kissed each other. I'm to take most of the blame for that as the guy is generally supposed to make the first move. It's not as if I didn't want to kiss Becca; I just didn't really know how or when to do it. Unfortunately, my time ran out as she eventually broke up with me. Did my disability have anything to do with the breakup? I honestly don't think it had any direct impact. Indirectly though, it had a large impact on our relationship. Since this was my first dating experience, I found out I'd have to always be thinking and staying one step ahead of the game. For example, if there was a party coming up, I'd have to start thinking about plans as far as how to get there, how to get inside, what other friends of mine would be there to help should I fall down or get knocked over, and other issues normally a guy wouldn't have to consider. As much as a relationship needs to have spontaneity, I needed to have things planned out well in advance.

Even though our relationship together wasn't some huge love story, it taught me a lot. It was one more stepping stone towards helping me realize that there are girls that can see past a physical disability and fall for a guy due to what he can offer from the inside. I've often thought that had we not dated at that point, and instead dated each other a couple of years later, we might have had something more special. I can't speak for Becca, but I just don't think I was really mature enough to handle some of the things that came up. We never became enemies and stayed friendly with each other throughout high school, but I've always been curious as to whether she might have had the same thoughts as far as our dating experience was concerned.

CHAPTER 7

IF LAURA Fajardo was my fantasy date and Becca Ligon was my first girlfriend, then Mandy Berden was my first true love.

I met Mandy in the eighth grade in U.S. History class. We sat totally on the opposite side of the classroom from each other, but that didn't mean I didn't notice her. Her best friend, Sara, was in the class, and Mandy always seemed to be following her lead. A friend of mine was also in that class, and he was good friends with Sara. So before class would start, I'd naturally hang around him in hopes that Sara would come over, with of course Mandy by her side. This plan worked, except there was one problem. Sara wouldn't shut up long enough for me to ever start any kind of conversation with Mandy. I wasn't confident enough to just start talking to Mandy on my own, so I took what I could get.

As any eighth-grade boy who is interested in a girl would do, I found out Mandy's class schedule and figured the path she would take before and after classes. Some people may call this the first steps or signs of stalking; I simply call it being a normal hormone-raged teenager. I made it a point to see Mandy "by chance" each day and at least say hi to her. As I've mentioned, the act of flirting was not something I ever struggled with. It was going beyond the flirt and capitalizing on it where I struggled.

Nothing happened between Mandy and me that year. I guess you could say we became friends, but outside of school we had no interaction with each other. At the time, our junior high school was the largest, as far as total number of students, in the whole state of Michigan, so a new school was built and opened going into our ninth grade year. Being that Mandy and I lived on opposite sides of town, we went to different junior highs as freshmen. The year went by, and I basically forgot about Mandy; Laura made that easy to do! There was still just one public high school, so after being split up for a year, our class came back together as sophomores.

Mandy and I ended up having our sophomore civics class together. It was our last class of the day, which allowed for some extended conversations after the bell rang. The desks were arranged so they were split down the middle by an open aisle with both sides facing the center of the room, as opposed to the front of the class. Mandy and I sat on opposite sides of the aisle, but were positioned so we both could look directly at each other. It didn't take long for me to start the games. Let me just say that I was pulling out all my tricks, and they seemed to be working. I had never had a girl so blatantly flirt right back at me. I was taken aback, but boy did I like it.

When I first met Mandy in junior high, she was good looking, but she wasn't the first girl your eyes would be drawn to out of a large group of people. Two years later, and now we're talking about the type of girl that makes guys do double-takes. This was no longer cute little Mandy; this was fully developed Mandy with curves in all the right places.

Our high school was designed with multiple buildings on campus, so you actually had to walk outside the majority of time to get from class to class. It wasn't exactly the layout of most common sense when you figure this was Northern Michigan we're talking about. In order to get to classes on time and not risk getting knocked over en route, I was using a power wheelchair for the first time at school, although I'd still get out of the chair once I got to a classroom. The wheelchair actually never even went past the entrance in our house. At that point in my life a wheelchair wasn't something that had any kind of positive connotation associated with it. It was a symbol of what my parents and I could see only as bad things to come.

The classroom next to the one I had civics with Mandy was empty during that period, so I would keep the wheelchair in there to allow for some more room in our class. Even though I knew she knew I was using the wheelchair, I made every possible effort to make sure Mandy never saw me in it before or after class. It wasn't that hard to pull off, as I'd wheel into the empty classroom, struggle to get myself up on my feet, and then slip into our class on foot. After class I'd usually talk for a few minutes with Mandy right outside the class doorway. Once we said good-bye, I'd make sure she had left the building, since our classroom was the first one inside the entrance, and then I'd take the couple of steps to the class where the wheelchair was stored and hop in to get ready to head home. I honestly had no clue how much Mandy knew about my disease; as far as I was concerned, the less the better.

My only previous dating experience had been with Becca, and that didn't turn out how I had wanted. Through all of the flirting, Mandy and I had really become good friends, and I didn't want to risk losing that friendship with a failed dating relationship—at least that's how I was justifying not asking her out on a date. This truly was the first time I had felt so strongly about a girl where it seemed the same was being reciprocated. What was holding me back? Why couldn't I simply ask her out on a date? I was coming up with every single excuse possible to justify my lack of action. The toughest part of all was that I felt there really wasn't somebody I could go to for advice. There was nobody in my community I knew of that had gone through the same thing. I wanted to ask my brother about normal dating experiences, but to my knowledge he hadn't gone out on any dates and now was away at his first year of college at the University of Kansas. For any child, it is difficult asking parents for initial dating advice, and I knew matters would be even more complicated for me due to the whole disability issue. My parents are the most supportive parents a son could ever ask for, but I had a feeling they would try to minimize the disability issue and just encourage me go for it, have fun, and let whatever was meant to be, happen. If it was only that simple.

Even though I didn't do anything to act on my emotions for the rest of that school year, it was in the cards for Mandy and me to be a couple. Our high school had a program called Cadet Teaching, in which students could sign up and receive credit for going to a nearby elementary school and assisting in a classroom for an hour during the day. My mom taught at a nearby elementary school that participated in this program, and she showed me a list of names of people that had signed up. Since it was optional for teachers to participate, my mom wanted to know if I knew anybody on the list and what my opinion was as to how they would be in a classroom of second graders. Well what name jumped out at me, but none other than Miss Mandy Berden. Trying my best not to be too obvious with my hidden motivation, I gave a glowing report and told my mom she needed to go in the next day and make sure she reserved or signed up Mandy. The wheels were in motion!

This was the perfect situation for me. You have to realize the type of personality my mom has. She is the kind of person that could hold a conversation with a cement wall and is able to find out every detail about a person's life in a blink of the eye. There isn't a question she is afraid to ask, and somehow she is able to get the most intimate details from people without them feeling uncomfortable or interrogated. If you're looking to get some rest on an airplane, you don't want my mom sitting next to you.

Even though I had gotten to know Mandy quite well, I knew this was going to be an opportunity that was really going to work to my advantage. I had my own personal spy that didn't even know she was doing spy work for me. Every day I would come home and get the "Mandy Report". I was able to learn about her family, hobbies, future aspirations, and most importantly, about her dating or boyfriend situation. Apparently Mandy wasn't dating anybody, or at least that's what she told my mom.

It was also a great way for Mandy to learn about me, not by her asking my mom questions, but simply by being in her classroom. My mom would tell her students all about our family, and they loved hearing all about what was going on in our lives. She did an unbelievable job of educating her students about disabilities and had a way of explaining my disability in the simplest terms, yet with enough information to satisfy their young, inquiring minds. This was the perfect way for Mandy to learn some of the basics of my disability while not having it all thrown in her face at once or by getting the wrong information through a different source. She would be able to hear through my mom that I was just like every other high school student and enjoyed participating in the same activities everybody else was involved in; it was just that I had some extra challenges most students didn't have to deal with. I couldn't have asked for a better situation.

At school, I was on the Junior Class Council, and it was sort of understood that everybody in student government would attend the homecoming dance in the fall. For weeks I had known I wanted to ask Mandy, but I still couldn't work up the onions to do so. Apparently nobody had asked Mandy yet, as I found out through my mom, who amazingly still hadn't figured out I really had a thing for this girl.

With less than a week to go before the dance, I knew I couldn't wait any longer. After getting home from school, I started to plot my game plan for the phone call. Every guy knows what I'm talking about. It's not just a simple matter of picking up the phone, dialing the number, and asking a girl out. There are tons of variables that must be anticipated and rehearsals that must take place. I could probably make a million dollars if I was able to develop a diagram or flow chart telling how to handle these situations for guys. The problem is that no matter how much guys rehearse or anticipate conversations, we still don't really understand how the female brain works and can be thrown for a loop by the simplest unexpected comment. If it wasn't anticipated, all of a sudden we travel back in time and have the brain and speech capacity of a Neanderthal.

The initial hello or greeting is very important. No matter who answers the phone, you should ask for the girl by name, even if you are 100% positive she is the one who answered the phone. I got myself in trouble not following this advice once as I assumed it was the girl I was trying to call, when in all actuality it ended up being her younger brother I was talking to! Should somebody else answer and say she is not available, it is vital you decide beforehand if you are going to leave a message and your number, or if you are simply going to say you'll try calling back later. If you don't have all of this planned out ahead of time, it can lead to some awkward pauses and give off the impression to her family that you are some sort of shy or wimpy boy, and without a doubt, they will tease her before you've even had an opportunity to talk with her.

After rehearsing my phone call multiple times and sequestering myself in my room so nobody would be able to hear me, I started to dial Mandy's phone number, stopping just before entering the last digit. I had never done this before and knew if I was ever going to ask a girl out on my own, things couldn't be aligned more perfectly than they currently were. Like somebody getting ready to test to see if a burner is still hot, I slowly moved my finger closer to the phone and quickly pushed the final number as if I was expecting to receive a shock in return. In the new day of caller ID, there was no looking back.

The conversation went nothing like I had rehearsed. I was jumping from one thing to the next and stumbling over all my words. I was losing control of the conversation and knew if I didn't quickly get to the point of asking Mandy to the dance, we would hang up, and it would be even harder for me to ask her later on. After an awkward pause and some silence, the words finally shot out of my mouth: "Do you want to go to the homecoming dance?"

Her response was music to my ears. It was as if she had been expecting me to ask her all along and she had already decided to say yes. She did realize she was saying "yes" to go with me, didn't she? I didn't specifically state that when I asked her. Thinking back, I had just asked if she had wanted to go to the dance . . . in general! When she inquired if we would be going with a group or just the two of us, I knew we were on the same page.

I don't know who was more shocked, my mom or me, when I told her I had asked Mandy to the homecoming dance and she had said yes. I'm not going to go as far as saying she felt Mandy was out of my league, but the look in her eyes told me she was proud of me for having the courage to finally ask somebody out, yet alone someone like Mandy. The look of shock and her smile quickly turned into a gasp when I told her the dance was less than a week away. She wanted to know why I had waited so long if

I had known I wanted to ask Mandy in the first place. I didn't really have a great answer, so I quickly tried to reroute the conversation towards dinner plans and attire for the evening.

The whole night ended up being wonderful—well, almost the whole night. We went to dinner with a group of friends and danced, in my own awkward yet stylish way, throughout the evening. We must have drawn more of an audience than I realized because the following week at school quite a few teachers commented by saying they saw me on the dance floor. For one of the first times in my life I wasn't ashamed or embarrassed by people saying they saw me participate in something in my own adaptive way. Instead, I was simply happy I could be out there with Mandy. She had a way of helping me be comfortable with myself like nobody had ever been able to do before. My self-esteem was rising to levels it never had approached. The evening ended in perfect fashion as I ended up kissing Mandy at her front door, saying goodnight.

I had gone over the process in my head a million times so that the awkwardness of the situation would be kept at a minimum, or at least in theory. Kevin had driven us, along with his date; I had told him ahead of time to be sure to let me out of our van, as I was in my wheelchair, so I could "walk" Mandy to her door. You had to walk around the side of her driveway and garage to get to the front door, so I figured there wouldn't be an audience when we got there. Once we rounded the corner of the garage, her front porch lights came on. All I could think was that her dad was going to show up standing in the door and ruin my master plan. Nonetheless, until somebody told me to leave, I still had one more thing to accomplish. By scooting forward and tilting the power seat in my wheelchair back, I was still able to get to my feet and stand. I told Mandy I had a great time and without hesitation leaned in for the hug and kiss.

To my excitement, there seemed to be no pull back or look of displeasure coming from her. It ended up being our first of countless kisses.

The adrenaline must have really been pumping inside of me, because as I went to sit back down in my wheelchair and was returning the seat to the normal level position, I lost my balance. Luckily I didn't fall, but I got stuck with my butt on the edge of the seat and my upper body fully bent forward looking down at my feet planted in front of me on the ground. Would my perfect night all of a sudden turn into a nightmare? I didn't have the strength to get my trunk back in an upright position and had to ask Mandy to push me back up. She did so, and knowing at this point to ask for a thank-you kiss was pushing things, I told her thanks, I'd see her at school, and was on my way back to the van.

For the rest of the weekend, I could only think of two things: our kiss and my crash-course method of welcoming Mandy to the world of dating somebody with a disability. Which would Mandy grab onto? Would she be the type of person who was able to accept the challenges that would go along with dating somebody in a wheelchair, or would she rather just be friends and enjoy our one date and leave it at that? Her huge smile and touch of her hand answered all my concerns as she met me before classes the following Monday.

The lights that came on when I walked Mandy back to her door after our first date were hooked up to sensors which were activated by our movement. Mandy told me about them months later!

CHAPTER 8

CRACK . . . IT was a sound I had never heard before, yet I knew instantly what it was. I just wasn't sure what it would mean for me in the long run.

May 23 is a day I've always had marked on my calendar because it's Kevin's birthday, but now Tuesday, May 23, 1995, would have even more significance for me. I had just gotten home along with my family from being over at the Sonnemanns, celebrating Kevin's 18th birthday. It was a tradition that had begun once Kevin and I had gotten too old to have the regular birthday party with classmates, cake, ice cream, and games.

Back at home, I was walking out of my bedroom to the bathroom across the hall to take a shower when my foot caught the corner of the door frame. Falling was obviously nothing new to me, and I had developed a way to do it so I would land in the least painful way. Picture somebody that has staged a fall for one of those funniest home video contests with arms flailing all over the place and body collapsing like jell-o; that's how I always envisioned myself looking. Well, the hallway wasn't wide enough to let me tuck and roll, so my fall consisted of the entire weight of my body landing on top of my right leg which got caught underneath me. I heard the bone snap, a gruesome sound if you've never heard a bone break, but I didn't really want to believe what I knew had just happened.

As was the normal routine for when I would fall, my dad came over and started to untangle the human pretzel I had formed. My scream of pain stopped his attempt to straighten me out. It wasn't the first time, and unfortunately, it wouldn't be the last time, my dad would look into my eyes and read the thoughts that were rushing through my mind, thoughts that had nothing to do with the pain I was in. Somehow he knew even though I was lying on the ground in agony, with what would end up being a fractured right femur, I was actually thinking about Mandy and how she would react to knowing her boyfriend would not be able to take her to the prom that was just a matter of days away. Even though I don't always share as many things with my dad as I do with my mom, he has a way of knowing my inner-most thoughts when all the cards are on the table.

It didn't take long for my parents to realize I was seriously hurt and they were not going to be able to move me on their own. Little did I know that the pain I was in while on the ground would hardly compare to what I was in store for. My mom dialed 911, and I remained on the ground wearing only my tightie-whities, not knowing what was in my near future.

Looking back on that fall, it marked quite a few firsts and lasts for me. It was my first broken bone, first ambulance ride, and first extended hospital stay that was non-MD related. It was also the last time I would walk unassisted anywhere, the last time I would talk to most people at eye level, and the last time I would wear tightie-whities! From that point forward, it was easier to go to the bathroom using a urinal and open fly most boxers have compared to the closed fronts of briefs. To this day, by the way, I'm still disappointed the ambulance never had to turn on the siren on the way to the hospital!

Pain is never fun, and it always puts things in perspective. I can't imagine having a disability or disease that also is associated with having pain on a daily basis. If I had to come up with one positive of MD, it's that there is no pain associated with it. Sure my body fatigues much quicker, but for the most part, it feels just like a healthy body, at least as far as I know; it just can't operate or perform like a normal body.

As I lay on the emergency room table, I felt like I was going to vomit on the spot as they moved my leg around attempting to reset it. Remember, the femur is the biggest bone in your body, and I had just broken it in three places with what's termed a spiral fracture. Picture a drinking straw that has been twisted or bent, resulting in cracks down the sides. That's what happened to my femur in three places. The sensation was that I had just turned into Gumby in my right leg, and it could be bent in any and every direction. The difference, though, is Gumby must not have any nerve endings or feeling, because I sure didn't have a big red smile plastered all over my face.

David was in the emergency room with me and was originally instructed to hold my foot in the air and in place while the techs manipulated my leg back to as straight as possible. Many times would arise in the future when I'd see first-hand my brother's true love for me, but this was one of the first times where our relationship grew without either one of us having to say a thing. Knowing he was hurting me was too much for him to handle. He physically couldn't deal with having to keep my foot from moving, seeing how much pain that gave me. I don't remember who ended up having to hold my foot; I just remember it wasn't David.

I will also never forget Kevin came to visit me that night in the emergency room. Here it was now past midnight, technically the next day after his birthday, and he's visiting his friend in the emergency room. To this day, I still wonder how much guilt he puts on his birthday and the fact it is also the "anniversary" of my broken leg and last time I was fully ambulatory; I put none. We all play the "what-if" game, so I'm sure it has crossed his mind many times. What if that night hadn't been his birthday? Would I still have tripped at home and broken my leg? Probably not, because I was a good couple of hours later than normal going through my night-time routine. Was a fall going to happen to me somewhere down the road with the same results? I can't answer that question for sure, but the answer is more than likely, "yes."

Knowing how stubborn I can be and how much I always push myself, the natural transition of walking and progressing into a wheelchair would not have been something I would have embraced. I'm fairly sure if it hadn't been for that fall, it would have taken another serious accident for me to switch over and become a fulltime wheelchair user. To this day, I've told people I would never wish a broken bone on anybody; but for me, in the long run, it might have been the best thing. It took the decision-making process out of the equation for me. I no longer had to listen to doctors or family members try to suggest it might be in my best interest to use a wheelchair every now and then. I mean, come on, who wants to have to make that choice, especially during your high school years when the most important thing is your impression of what other people think of you. At that point in my life, I couldn't have named to you one person who was or had been a wheelchair user, yet alone anybody in my school or community. Unfortunately, to this day there still aren't many famous faces that come to mind when thinking of Hollywood and physical disabilities. Don't get me wrong, I'm not saying that I'm wishing for some stars to be diagnosed with all these terrible disabilities that result in having to use a wheelchair. I just wish it would become more common to see people in wheelchairs on TV shows and movies.

One of the great things about having parents who were both public school teachers in a relatively small community is that they either knew or had some connection with just about everyone in town. One of the worst things about having parents who were both public school teachers in a relatively small community is that they either knew or had some connection with just about everyone in town! This time it would prove to be a major blessing. The initial orthopedic surgeon who was on duty ended up not being a good match. My parents were still acting on my behalf at that point, since I was a minor, and luckily they were able to talk and make decisions for me. This guy just wanted to get me into the operating room, cut me open, and send me on my way as if I was just any ordinary patient with a broken leg. If there is one thing I am not, it is ordinary, especially when dealing with anything in the medical arena. There has to be consultation with my neuromuscular disease doctor, major consideration for which type of anesthesia to use, as caution has to be given for any type of drug that might cause malignant hyperthermia, resulting in total paralysis, a common side effect for patients with DMD while under anesthesia. I require a special bed while in the hospital, so I don't develop pressure sores, since I am not able to turn myself on my own. Where and how the rehab and physical therapy process will take place needs to be determined. There is just a huge list of items I need to consider and figure out that the normal patient doesn't even have to consider. This first doctor didn't see my situation as being any different.

It was at that point when my parents knew we had to contact somebody who had a personal knowledge of my medical situation and would take the extra precautionary steps necessary to secure my health and safety. My parents first talked with our minister and close friend Dr. Gary Hogue, who gave us a recommendation. That's when Dr. Edward Brophy entered into my life. It proved to be one of a couple of recommendations I would receive after my fracture, in which new people would enter into my life and have huge impacts towards making me the person I am today.

After consulting with Dr. Mendell at Ohio State, Dr. Brophy carefully constructed our game plan. Casting my leg wouldn't be an option as that would require me to be immobile for too long, causing too much muscle atrophy. We had no idea what my future was as far as being able to walk again, but every effort would be made to get me back to where I was before the fall. Right away, I knew I liked Dr. Brophy and how he was handling my case. My parents were also comforted that he was taking extra time to explain all the possible options and was doing research on his own to be able to recommend what he felt was my best route. Collectively we decided to opt for surgery, inserting a titanium rod into my femur and attaching it with multiple screws at the top and bottom of the bone. This would let me move around sooner than other options and allow me to start rehab quicker, which would hopefully reduce atrophy.

What I really appreciated about Dr. Brophy was that he was taking the time to try to get to know me as a person, not just as another patient. First of all, he wanted to know about my daily routines. He realized any change in my strength and ability would have a huge impact on how I would get through a day. He wanted to make every effort possible to keep me as active as I had been. Second, he wanted to know about my social life. He wanted to know what I did for fun and to find a way for me to get out of the hospital as soon as possible so I could enjoy life again. He knew how serious my accident was and how depression could easily set in if I was stuck in a hospital room or at home without having other things going on in my life to cheer me up. He truly was looking at the whole broken picture and wanted to play a part in putting the puzzle back together.

During one of our first discussions following surgery, I told Dr. Brophy that for the last couple of months I had been planning the prom at my high school. I was president for the junior class, and the major responsibility of the junior class was always to plan and put on that year's prom. I was the head coordinator and now had to rely on my committee members to not only follow through with everything that had been assigned to them, but also to kick it up a notch to replace my leadership. There really wasn't much Dr. Brophy could do to help me with that situation, but there was one major dilemma hanging over my head that I had high hopes he could help me with. I needed to be able to take Mandy to the prom. She was so excited for it and had been anticipating everything for so long. The dress had been bought, hair and nails appointment set, dinner reservations made—everything was in order—until her boyfriend had to go and break his leg!

I really didn't think there would be any way I'd be discharged within four days following surgery, in time to go. Even if I was discharged, I seriously doubted a prom would be in my rehab papers. Well, that's when I found out Dr. Brophy was not only my new orthopedic surgeon, but he was also my new advocate. Upon hearing my wish, he made that goal number one. Together we would do everything it took in order for me to attend the prom.

Flash forward four days following surgery to the morning of Sunday, May 28. In came Dr. Brophy to do what I was hoping to be my final examination before getting my discharge papers. I still was in disbelief this might actually occur. Pain continued to be a major part of my day, but I was doing everything in my power to mask it. Apparently, I was able to hide it enough because I was cleared to leave the hospital. In all reality, I'm quite sure it would have been in my best interest to stay in the hospital a little bit longer. As far as my other interests went, getting out of that place was the sweetest thing I had heard since falling.

The countdown was on. Noon was quickly approaching and my to-do list was looking quite full. First was to have my parents run back to our house to get some clothes for me to put on to get back home in. While they were doing that, I would call Mandy to let her know she did have a date for the prom and our plans were a go . . . for the most part. Originally, Kevin was going to drive us along with his date to meet with a small group of friends for dinner before heading to the dance. That part was out of the question as I just wouldn't be able to physically handle it. My dad would have to drive us, which wasn't my first choice, but it would have to do. My parents were already going to be chaperones for the prom, so it's not as if I wouldn't have seen them anyway. It wasn't Mandy's first choice either, but at this point she'd take what she could get.

My parents finally returned to my hospital room, and now it was time to get dressed and head home. Easier said than done. Remember, I had been in the hospital for the last four days, so I'd just been wearing my hospital gown. All of a sudden, underwear and pants had been thrown back into the equation. Luckily my parents brought a pair of athletic style shorts for me to put on. After struggling to get them all the way up, while doing what seemed like an hour of mini-rolls on each side, it was time to transfer out of bed and into my wheelchair. We had prepared for this situation as we'd gotten a leg extender for the right leg rest of my wheelchair. At this point in my recovery, it was too painful for me to have my leg bent at the knee in a normal seated position for any prolonged length of time. I needed to have it fully extended, preferably secured in its brace or immobilizer.

The next step would be the van ride home. None of us had actually thought about trying to fit into the back of our van with my leg fully extended. This was tougher than trying to parallel park a SUV into a spot made for a go-cart. After multiple attempts, I finally was in position and ready to head home. Was it really just four days ago that I had gotten back from Kevin's birthday party and was walking? So much can change in such a little amount of time. If I didn't know that already, all the bumps during the ride home certainly reminded me.

If you've never been in a hospital for an extended period, let me tell you that sponge baths aren't all they're cracked up to be. There are multiple reasons why: the first being that they aren't the sexual fantasy you see played out in the movies. Simply getting cleaned is the main reason. There are certain areas that get cleaned in a shower or tub that just don't get cleaned as well while in bed with a rag. Odors seem to build without you really knowing it. Your skin gets all dry and cracked, and you start to peel in places you didn't even know you could peel. Your hair gets really oily and your scalp becomes super itchy.

Start Extreme Makeover: Male Prom Edition. I couldn't believe all the products my mom had brought out for me to use. Our kitchen had become my own personal health spa area. I wasn't allowed to shower yet; and even if I had been, there was no way I was physically going to be able to take on that event. When you have a disability, being creative becomes second nature. If you can't get into a shower to wash your hair, you come up with the next best alternative: the kitchen sink and extendable hose sprayer. I tilted my chair and backed up to the sink to get my hair washed. Hey, if Mandy was going to pay big bucks and get all made over at her salon, I would try to take advantage of everything that Gerhardt Spa & Kitchen would have to offer. I was even thinking of going for the deluxe package and asking for a turkey sandwich.

All right, I was all washed up and actually smelled pretty good. My dad had splashed a little cologne on me, as if I needed anything else to get me a little higher and light headed. Everything had been done except for one last task: my tuxedo. My parents and I both knew it wasn't on yet, but nobody wanted to be the first to say anything about it. We knew how difficult it had been just to put on a pair of slippery loose shorts at the hospital while in bed. Putting on a pair of tuxedo pants while in my wheelchair seemed more daunting than cutting the toenails of a squirming baby. After a few futile attempts and screams of pain, it was decided I would attend prom the way every guy dreams of going . . . in shorts! I still put on my tuxedo shirt, vest, jacket, and bow tie, but stayed in my shorts. Now remember these weren't your ordinary khaki or dress shorts; they were athletic shorts and a mix between teal and green in color nonetheless. Sure, my dad could have brought my black ones for me to put on coming home, but no, he had to pick my teal pair. If nothing else, the era was captured forever in the pictures taken due to the style and color of those shorts.

My dad drove me to Mandy's house early so pictures could be taken, and then we came back to our house to do the whole picture thing all over again. What is it with dates and moms when it comes to pictures? Of all the pictures taken pre-prom of the two of us, of the two of us with my parents, of the two of us with her parents, of the two of us with my parents and her parents, of the two of us with my parents and our new puppy—inside, outside, holding hands, not holding hands—I'm sure there were over one hundred taken! When we were all done, there was a constant white light that kept flashing in my vision. The only problem was that I didn't know if it was due to all the flashes from cameras or the wonderful pain medication I was taking at every available opportunity.

I wish I could tell you more about the remainder of that night, but in all honesty, it was one big blur. I do remember getting lots of high-fives from other guys who were all jealous they couldn't also be in shorts. The decorations looked great, and I couldn't have been more proud of the prom committee and all they accomplished with me being in the hospital. I hope Mandy had a good time, even if it wasn't all she had originally hoped for. I know it wasn't how I had wished for things to go, but thanks to Dr. Brophy, an awful situation turned out as positively as possible. If nothing else, it sure was memorable!

CHAPTER 9

MANDY AND I would continue to date throughout high school and really had a storybook senior year as she was named Senior Homecoming Queen, and I was named Homecoming King. While many people look back on their high school years and say it was an awkward time and one they'd rather forget, mine was in total contrast. My time in high school was the best period of my life. It could have been the worst as it also was the time I transitioned from walking to using a wheelchair, but my core of friends really pulled me through and mentally helped me.

Mandy and I were inseparable. My parents even ended up getting me my own phone line in my bedroom as we were on the phone so much with each other. If I ever thought somebody couldn't love me due to my disability, Mandy taught me otherwise. I truly thought she was the one and we'd live together happily ever after as high school sweethearts. We talked about our future plans and fantasized about our future house and kids together. I knew she was my first true love and was convinced we'd always be together.

High school graduation came along with my acceptance into Michigan State University. Mandy was a little unsure about her college plans at that point, and ultimately decided to stay in town and attend our local community college. Everybody told us long-distance relationships don't work, and they all had their horror stories, but I was convinced we could make it. Mandy initially thought it would be best if we separated, but I wasn't about to have anything to do with that. Should things not work out, they don't work out, but I wasn't going to call things off simply because it was the easy thing to do and due to others saying we wouldn't be able to make it work.

To say it was easy would be a lie. We struggled that first year apart and had quite a few ups and downs, but we made it through our freshman year of college apart, and I came back home for the summer. If I had any doubts that we were meant to be together, they were wiped away after surviving our year apart from each other. I wasn't ready to ask her to marry me, but looking at rings together certainly wouldn't be out of the question, or so I thought.

The summer started off great as we were initially spending every possible minute together. Mandy ended up working at a summer day camp held at the elementary school where my mom taught. Ironically, it was my mom that told Mandy about the job opening because one of her friends was in charge of the hiring process.

As the weeks went by, I noticed our time together was becoming a little less frequent as she was spending more time with her co-workers and friends she had made at her work. I initially thought nothing of it and actually felt it was a good thing, because it allowed me to spend some time with my other friends who were home for the summer. Those feelings soon turned to concerns, as friends kept asking me, "Who is this guy we keep seeing Mandy with?" Multiple people said they had seen her either out boating, roller-blading, or in a car with another guy on various occasions.

Of course this concerned me, but I told myself not to overreact and that I could trust Mandy.

Eventually I was fed up with people asking me what was going on, so I decided to ask Mandy about it. Even though I didn't like what I had been hearing and all it implied, I was confident there would be a reasonable answer and we'd be fine. After all, we had made it through our year apart, and this was supposed to be our summer back happy together.

The school and day camp were within walking distance in my wheelchair from my house, so I decided to go and surprise Mandy one day after work. She seemed a little flustered when she saw me, not like she was hiding something, but just not her normal self or that she was all that thrilled to be seeing me at that moment. I sort of hung back and allowed her to finish her duties and waited for all of the kids to leave. As we were walking to her car, the conversation was really awkward and was more like two people forced together, as opposed to two people who had been together for years. Before she got in her car, I looked her in the eye and said, "Mandy, I need to ask you something." She must have known where I was going, as her eyes instantly turned red and began to tear up. That was the beginning of the end as she didn't even have to say a thing for me to know what was coming next.

We didn't cut things off instantly. We still went out a few more times over the course of the next few weeks, but things just weren't the same as I knew she was seeing more and more of this "other guy". Ultimately, it was too much, and we officially broke up. Emotionally it was the hardest thing I have ever gone through. Call me naïve, but I honestly thought we would be together forever. I was a mess and couldn't understand what had gone wrong. All of my hopes and dreams hinged on the prospects of the two of us getting back together. I didn't want to leave the house or do anything with anybody. Everywhere I looked, I saw something from Mandy. Everywhere I went, something reminded me of our time together. I couldn't do anything without thinking of her. It affected me so much that I ended up going to a psychiatrist who clinically diagnosed me as going through a case of depression and put me on antidepressants.

I found it interesting how I could be diagnosed with a terminal disease and carry on with my life and look at it as more of a challenge than a setback, yet a broken heart was more than I could handle and required the use of medication to get back on track.

It's always interesting to be able to look back on events that occurred earlier in life and analyze them from a distance. As painful as our break-up was, I would never trade that experience along with all of the wonderful things we did and shared together. For that period of nearly three years, Mandy and I were meant to be together; we were meant to be a couple. Were we meant to be together forever? Apparently not, but that doesn't take anything away from the time we did have together. For better or worse, people change. It took me a long time to realize that, or maybe a better way of putting it is to say it took me a long time to accept that. It wasn't something I said or did; it was that Mandy had changed. I'm not even saying she changed for the worse; I'm simply saying her change didn't include me in it, at least as far as being in a relationship was concerned.

During the summer of 2006, we had our 10-year high school reunion, and I actually sat at the same table with Mandy and her husband—yes, the same guy whom she broke up with me for. It was at that point I realized I had completely gotten over her, and we finally had some closure.

She was the one for me earlier in my life, but not the present. I'm still looking for the one to live with the remainder of my life. One of my biggest unfulfilled dreams is to have a family of my own, which thanks to Mandy, I know will happen someday. She proved to me there are those in this world that have the special ability to see past a disability and recognize the true person I am and all I stand for.

At this point in my life, I'm through with the bar scene. I've also tried the online dating game but haven't had any success. I thought about not mentioning my disability or cropping my picture so it wouldn't include my wheelchair, but realized this would just be delaying the inevitable. If I wish to have a long-term relationship with somebody, it is going to have to be somebody that is comfortable with my disability and has an open mind. I know that person is out there; it's just a matter of God putting me in that right spot at the right time again. I've had enough time to be comfortable with myself on my own; I'm ready to take that next step in life and commit to a partnership and relationship for the long term.

CHAPTER 10

S OMETIMES THE toughest decisions in life are also the most obvious. I knew what I had to do, but making it official was extremely difficult. Deep down inside I knew what was best for me, but the alternative wasn't looking so bad . . . and would have been easier on every single person involved.

I applied only to one college. There was no point in spending the money on application fees to other places; I knew where I wanted to go. I wasn't worried about getting accepted. I met the entrance criteria above and beyond and my application was overflowing with extracurricular activities, not to mention a high school grade point average actually above a 4.0 on a 4.0 scale, due to taking advanced placement and honors courses. If I was going to go away to college, there was only one place for me: Michigan State University. Both of my parents graduated from MSU, and I was raised a Spartan. Growing up I even had MSU wallpaper in my bedroom. I cheered on the Spartans like no other. I had thought about also applying to the University of Pennsylvania, as I was planning on going into business and was curious to see whether or not I could get accepted at an Ivy League school, but I'm cheap and didn't want to spend the money!

I applied before the start of my senior year of high school and quickly received my early acceptance letter in the mail. Naturally, it was a big day, but only the start of what would become a grueling and stressful decision-making process of whether or not to accept the offer and opportunity. Moving away from home and going to college is a huge step in anybody's life. Add to it the daily struggles, both physical and mental, of having a disability, and it is challenging at the least, impossible for some. I knew if I wanted to continue to grow as a person and accomplish all of the professional goals I had set for myself, going away to college was something I had to try. I had never let a challenge get the better of me, and I wasn't about to start. Of course that was easy enough to say in my head, but to actually verbalize it and start the whole process was another ballgame.

There would be the obvious emotion of being homesick and not having somebody daily to look over me, but I would also be experiencing having somebody other than my parents take care of my physical and extremely up-close and personal needs. Since the fracture of my femur, I hadn't been away from the care of at least one of my parents for more than a single night.

There was also my relationship with Mandy to think about. She had toyed with the idea of going to Michigan State, but it really wasn't the place for her. The large campus was intimidating to her as she was looking to go to a smaller school. She was considering applying to Grand Valley State University, a smaller state college in Michigan located near Grand Rapids, but more than likely was going to stay in Traverse City and go to our local community college, Northwestern Community College.

I too could stay at home and go to NMC—sure, kids from our high school joked that it stood for No Man's College, but it did make a lot of sense. I could save lots of money, although my first year was basically paid for in academic scholarships to MSU. At home, I could get my basic university requirements completed to transfer later. I wouldn't have to leave Mandy, and we could throw out the window all of this talk and concern of whether or not we were going to give a long-distance relationship a chance. I also would still be able to live at home and not have to go through the process of having someone new take care of my physical needs. That was something that was scaring me and I didn't even know where in the process to begin to see if that was even a remote possibility. Overall, everything about attending NMC was easier. But easier isn't always better.

It took about a month, but I finally made my decision. I would pay my deposit and commit to being a Spartan for the fall of 1996. No, there wasn't a big press conference or news bulletin like they have for star sports recruits coming out of high school, but this was a huge moment. It was probably the biggest decision I had made up to that point in my life, if still not the biggest.

You would have thought I would have first announced my decision to my parents and if not them, then to Mandy, or at least my brother or Kevin. None of them made the cut. The first person I actually told my decision to was an old and trusted friend, Lori Warmbold, who at that time was starting her senior year at MSU. Lori was like, and still is, the big sister I never had growing up. Coincidently, she had also been a cadet teacher for my mom in her classroom, which is how I first met and developed a bond with her. As much as I had shied away from talking to my brother about girls or relationships, Lori had always been a listening ear for me. The reason I told her first was because I needed to get a reaction back that was 100% enthusiastic. From the beginning, Lori had always encouraged me to attend Michigan State and felt it was something I could physically undertake. She understood it wouldn't be easy, but then again, she knew taking the easy road just wasn't part of my way of doing things in life.

Sure, I could attend NMC for a couple of years and later transfer to MSU, but the longer I put off going away to college, the harder it would be to do in the future. I knew my parents would be excited to hear my news, but I also knew this was opening the doors to some of their biggest fears. Mandy would also be happy for me, but was this going to be the beginning of the end as far as our relationship together was concerned? I needed to tell somebody of my decision so I could move forward, and Lori was the right person at the right time.

It was truly a decisive spot in my life where I made the decision and commitment that my disease was not going to be the one thing to control my life. Of course it could place limitations on me, but limitations are only as constricting as one allows them to appear.

I had never heard of any stories of any young men with DMD attempting to move away and go to college. There were a couple I knew that attended schools located in their hometown or city, but nothing that involved moving away from the comfort and care of home and parents. There was no guide or action plan I could copy or even a person to talk to in order to avoid making some of the same mistakes.

My parents and I both knew that in order for this to work, it wasn't going to be something that was just going to fall into place on its own. It was going to have to be something that we researched, planned, and carefully oversaw right from the start.

The first thing we did was get in contact with what was then known as the Office of Programs for Handicapper Students (OPHS) at Michigan

State. Later on as a student, I would be part of an advisory committee that would make the recommendation to the President of the University to change the name of the office to the Resource Center for Persons with Disabilities (RCPD), not only to reflect a change in language, but also to allow faculty and staff with disabilities to utilize the resources the office provided on campus. The office staff was wonderful and really welcomed me as an incoming student. They wanted to personally know me, as well as to figure out what types of services I would be requesting or needing while on campus. I really had only three concerns when it came to my disability and the university: accessibility, transportation, and my personal health/daily living care.

As luck would have it, MSU was, and currently still is, one of the most accessible campuses in all of the Midwest. While it can't be considered a wheelchair utopia, each year the campus continues to make accommodations, accessibility, and campus climate a concerned topic. Even if I hadn't already decided to become a Spartan, MSU would have been towards the top of my list of colleges that would have been able to meet my accessibility concerns and needs.

I was promised that all of my accessibility and transportation needs on campus would be met. Should there be the slight possibility that I would be enrolled in a class that met in an inaccessible classroom, it would be immediately moved to an accessible one, no questions asked. Most of the buildings on campus were equipped with power-operated doors, with more in the plans to be converted every future semester. As long as I registered as a "handicapper" student on campus, I would be eligible to receive door-to-door para-transit bus transportation to all of my classes by just purchasing a regular student bus pass. Yes, this would mean riding in another "short bus", the stereotypical mode of transportation for people with cognitive disabilities and something everybody that uses a wheelchair experiences, but it sure would beat trying to navigate campus outdoors during Michigan winters. I would be able to have a low sodium diet specially prepared for me in my dorm cafeteria so that the normal freshman "fifteen" didn't balloon up to the freshman "forty". The only area OPHS couldn't assist me with was my health care or daily living needs, the biggest thing holding me back!

I understood why; they had legal concerns. Not only were there issues on my side—trusting somebody with a key to my room, not being physically violated, paying somebody and the tax issues, amongst others—but there were also factors for the person doing the care. If he or she were to get injured while helping me, who would be responsible for that person's medical costs? There were many factors to consider, and it had been the office's experience to let students handle that situation on their own rather than to also get involved. While my initial contact with OPHS was positive and the initial ground work had been laid, my biggest challenge of finding the consistent care I would require day in and day out was still unsolved.

My senior year in high school came and went, and still nothing had been resolved as far as figuring out what to do about my living situation. I went down to East Lansing in the spring with my parents before classes let out for the summer at MSU. We posted flyers across campus and put an ad in the school newspaper. Students weren't really looking that far ahead for a job of that nature for the fall, so we didn't receive a single response.

Amongst her friends, my mom isn't afraid to talk about anything. Oftentimes this can be embarrassing, but other times it can lead to answers to problems that may otherwise go unsolved. This ended up being one of those times.

My mom happened to be getting her nails done, or I guess a manicure is the correct term, and was talking with her nail technician about my current dilemma and how stressful the situation was becoming for our family. At first, this always struck me just as my mom being herself and talking about anything and everything, but I guess it was no different than some of the conversations men have at a barber shop while getting their hair cut. Anyway, her nail lady said that she had another client who had a son, Chris, who was already a student at MSU and was looking to get into the medical field. After mentioning the family's name, my mom was shocked because she knew them. Chris' grandmother had actually babysat my brother David for a year before he started nursery school.

My mom called the mother and described my situation. She talked to Chris, and he seemed interested. A time was set up for him to come to our house to get to know me, and basically to see if this was something that he would be interested and willing to commit to full time. I don't know if I would have labeled it as an interview, but it was a chance to see if our personalities would click or clash.

I didn't know what to expect upon meeting Chris, but it's a good thing I didn't let my very first impression get the best of me. I was sitting at home looking out our dining room window, which looks out onto our driveway. Out of nowhere, I hear a loud rumble as a motorcycle came streaking into view with a rider all decked out in leather, and then parked in our driveway. Nothing against people that ride motorcycles or wear leather, but it just wasn't the picture I had in my head for what Chris was going to look like.

Here's the funny part. Of all the stereotypes you can place on motorcycle riders, Chris ended up being about as opposite as they come. Describing him as rough and tough would be like saying a little bunny rabbit is big and scary; they just don't go together. After getting to know Chris, you'd say he'd be more likely to be driving a Volkswagen Beetle with decals on the doors and corny bumper stickers than a motorcycle. First impression aside, Chris and I hit it off.

He was everything that I was looking for. A couple of years older than I, he was fully set in his educational path and wasn't into the party scene anymore, yet he was still going to be at MSU beyond just one more year. He was strong and a male—two things that are tough to find together when looking for health care. He didn't mind the hours required for the position, and he was still going to be living in the dorms on campus, not in a house or apartment off campus. I was later able to get my room assignment changed so that I would be living in the same residence hall as Chris, which made things even more convenient for the two of us.

Chris had gone to the same high school in Traverse City as I. He was between the ages of my brother and me, so we had a lot of acquaintances and even some of the same friends. From something that had been freaking me out, with a deadline quickly approaching, Chris was starting to ease some of my largest concerns. I could also see a look of hope and promise in my parents' eyes.

The greatest compliment I can give any care provider is to be first thought of as a friend and then as an employee. That's exactly how I ended up thinking of Chris, and still do. All I can do is let out a little laugh when I think back on our times together. Not only will I never forget the displeasure of having to wake up to the odor of his coffee breath every morning, or the fun of teasing him about cranking up the volume on my TV due to his poor hearing to about twice the level I'd have it at, but I'll never forget how he made my dream of going away to college not only a possibility, but a reality. Chris is a perfect example of how somebody totally out of the blue can drop-in on your life and impact it in ways that can't be calculated.

The summer between graduating from high school and being a freshman in college is a memorable one. For the first time, you start thinking of yourself truly as an adult and feeling that others are also looking at you differently. Of course, as you get even older and look back at yourself, you realize you were just as immature as ever, if not more, but that's what makes you feel so knowledgeable at the time.

The summer months passed swiftly, and the day to head down to MSU arrived. If a carload of tears were shed the day we left David at the University of Kansas, then this was a busload, and then some more; that's not to say I was the favorite child or anything like that. The difference was this was all of the exact emotions that were felt saying good-bye to David, plus all of the fears that my disability brought along with it.

I don't know if I've ever cried as much over a 48-hour period as I did those two days. Starting the whole trip off by having to say good-bye to Mandy was hell. Despite what everybody had said to us, we decided to give a long-distance relationship a try. If our reaction to just leaving was our first test, then this was going to be rough. Of course if leaving had turned out to be easy, then that would have been a sign that things weren't strong to begin with between us, and it wouldn't have been all that big of a deal. The drive down to campus was three hours, and I don't think I fully stopped crying until the very end of the drive.

As raw as my emotions were, I can only imagine what was going through the hearts and minds of my parents. The toughest thing for any parent to do is to let go and have their child grow and move on through life. This had to be beyond words, because not only did they have to let go, but they also had to allow somebody new to grab on. My daily care had suddenly been handed over to somebody who, just a couple of months before, none of us would have known had he been sitting at a table right next to us.

It was one of those experiences we all had hoped for and dreamed would one day come true, but now that the day had come, the reality of it all was almost too much to handle. Upon initially being diagnosed, I'm sure going away to college wasn't even something my parents felt would be a possibility. Just being able to go to school and have friends in regular classes seemed like a wish out of a lamp. Such a dismal picture had originally been painted that I'm sure at first my parents couldn't even think far enough down my road in life to consider the reality of college. According to textbooks and research journals of the day, I was lucky enough to simply be alive.

Before saying our final good-bye and leaving me on campus, my anxiety and stress had risen so high that I had literally made myself sick and nauseated. I had never experienced this much doubt, apprehension, or fear in my life. Had my parents said, "Let's forget about this and go home," I would have been the one leading the way to the car. Luckily they took a different approach. They didn't try to hide that they were just as scared, if not more, about the whole situation as I, but instead talked openly about their fears and how natural and valid it was for me to be feeling the same way. At the same time, they made sure to remind me of how going to college had always been a lifelong dream of mine and how I had never let DMD defeat me. They told me to look at the situation as one big experiment. The best thing about an experiment is that it can be changed as it moves forward. Nothing had to be set in stone. If I gave it a try and my best effort, nobody could ever say that I hadn't given it a shot.

Had I not even tried, for the rest of my life there would be that voice in the back of my head always asking and wondering what could have been.

I wasn't happy with the status-quo as far as my life was concerned at that point, and I'm still not today. I needed to move forward with my education and make myself more marketable and employable. It came down to making the decision of either moving forward in life and continuing on my quest to be as independent and "normal" as possible, or going back, living at home, and starting down the road of living my life with my disability as the focus and living off disability payments and part-time jobs. I knew I wanted more out of life than that, and owed it to myself to give it a try.

CHAPTER 11

"ABSENCE MAKES the heart grow fonder," according to the famous proverb. Growing up I never really thought that would be the case concerning the relationship between my brother and me. We had what I would classify as the typical brother relationship as kids. He was not quite three years older than I, so I was close enough in age where I could be with his friends and still be a part of their activities. From his point of view, I was just young enough where I could be a pain in the ass and bother him while he was with his friends!

I think both of us would admit we weren't all that close as kids. It's not as if we didn't get along or hated each other; we just had different personalities and interests. Other than sports, there wasn't much we'd talk about with each other. He'd pick on me as any big brother would do, but it never got the point where it was out of hand. We loved each other because we were brothers and were supposed to, but we each had our own lives.

We all take things for granted, and I remember the day I realized I had been taking my brother for granted. He had enrolled at the University of Kansas for his freshman year of college. The summer before leaving home, I knew things would be different, but I wasn't too concerned about missing

David. I was actually more concerned with how my parents would react to having their first child go away, leaving me at home alone with them. You have to realize how emotional my parents are, and I didn't know if being the only child at home was going to be a positive or negative experience. Would they tighten their grip even more and suffocate me as an only child, or would the reigns be let loose. I was pretty confident it would be the first, but I didn't know how different things would get.

The time finally came for David to leave. We all packed his stuff in our van and left together for what ended up being an experience that had a greater impact for each of us individually than what we could have imagined. After a 14-hour ride through the blazing summer heat and humidity only the great plains of the Midwest States can offer, we arrived in Lawrence, Kansas. We stayed overnight in a hotel; and following a day of unpacking and getting David settled in his dorm room, we started the process of saying our good-byes.

I say process because before anything else, you have to realize what a "Gerhardt Good-bye" is. It's not a simple wave, well wishes, pat on the back or hug, and turn and leave. It's a recap of the time just spent together with hopes of doing it again really soon and not just a blanket statement incorporating everything together; there are details involved. There are hugs and arms around shoulders and then more hugs. There's safety tips brought up if somebody is leaving or reassurance we'll be safe if we're doing the traveling. Oddly enough, there aren't awkward pauses or moments of silence; my mom makes sure to fill in all of those gaps. A quick rundown of luggage and supplies has to be done, if nothing else, just to use up a little more time before the actual departure actually takes place. A promise to call, once arrival at the point of destination has happened, is a must. After all of this has occurred, along with reassurance that the car has been filled with enough gas and windshield wiper fluid before having to get onto the highway, another set of hugs and kisses, before finally getting into the vehicle, is allowed. After starting the car, the window must be lowered and then a promise of safe driving—and a phone call will be made again. This is something that must be figured into a set of plans. If not, a trip can get off on the wrong foot as somebody is going to be late without taking the proper steps to incorporate a Gerhardt Good-bye into the itinerary.

This was one Gerhardt Good-bye I will always remember, not so much for what was or wasn't said, but for the huge emptiness and feeling as if I had just been punched in the gut. It wasn't supposed to be happening this way. If anything, I was supposed to be feeling a sense of joy. No longer was I going to have to put up with being poked and picked on. I wasn't going to have to share anything else around the house, and there was even talk of knocking down the wall that separated both of our bedrooms, making it one large room—all mine!

I can picture David standing next to where our van was parked as we pulled out of the parking lot. To be honest, he looked rather pathetic as he stood there in the 100-degree heat, holding a plastic bag from the store where he had just purchased a KU hat. Was he going to be all right? Was I going to be all right? Why was I even having these thoughts? It wasn't supposed to be this way. It was at that point—as my dad, mom, and I drove away—that it hit me how much I had looked up to my brother and how much I knew I could always rely on him to support and protect me. I was losing my security blanket.

I sat there and realized that I had never once seen or heard my brother do something to suggest he regretted having a brother with a physical disability. To this day, that still holds true. Kids can say things without fully thinking of the ramifications of their statements and have a way of putting their foot in their mouth every now and then. Not only did David never do this to me concerning my MD, but I never overheard him say anything out of frustration to my parents. What you see is what you get when it comes to David. He's not about playing games or putting up a front. The facts were that he had a younger brother with a disability, so he dealt with that and made the situation as normal as possible.

The emotions of siblings of somebody with a disability I'm sure are totally different than the feelings parents go through. Ever since my diagnosis, David has had to take a back seat or play second fiddle to me. It's normal practice when parents are talking to other parents to ask how their children are doing. I'll bet you nine times out of ten when my parents are talking to others, they'll be asked about how I am doing. Not "How are David and Mo doing?" but just, "How is Mo doing?" Now I don't blame these people, as their hearts are in the right place; my point is that being a sibling of somebody with a disability often puts you in the shadows. I'm sure this results in resentment and depression for many. Luckily, I think I can say that David never went through those stages, at least for any lengthy period of time.

A strange thing happened that first fall when we were apart from each other. We talked on the phone more than we had in person growing up together! It was as if all of a sudden not only were we brothers, but we were friends. We were talking to each other because we wanted to, not because we had to. I don't want to say going away to college changed my brother; because that makes it sound like it was totally his fault we weren't super close growing up, which it wasn't. Neither one of us was to blame; it's just how it was. The best part of it all is we've continued to grow closer since that experience.

School was always tough for my brother, but not due to a lack of effort or time put in to studying; academics just never came naturally to him.

While hitting a baseball was just second nature, getting good grades was a struggle. He wasn't a slacker or somebody who skipped classes all the time; he was the one that was always right in the middle. When class averages were set, that's more than likely right where he'd be.

Unfortunately, there was a physiology class he just couldn't get through for his major while at Kansas. After a couple of unsuccessful attempts and the cost of tuition increasing, David had the difficult task of having to tell my parents he was dropping out of college. I can't imagine how difficult this was for him. Keep in mind that both of our parents are school teachers and at this same point in time, I was at Michigan State making the Dean's List. To his credit, David packed his bags, came home and got a job to pay off some of his debt, and then continued his education by taking classes at the community college in our hometown. He knew that even though he hadn't been able to complete his education at the University of Kansas, he needed to get a college degree to be able to live the life he wanted to lead.

I have had enough experiences in my life to come to the realization that everything happens for a reason. At first we don't know what those reasons are, but when you're able to look back and see things from a distance, you're usually able to put the puzzle pieces together and see the grand picture. David dropping out from the University of Kansas was no exception. After successfully completing some courses at the community college, David knew it was time to go after his college degree one more time. To the thrill of all the Gerhardts, David made the announcement during the fall of 1998 that he had applied to Michigan State for the upcoming spring of 1999 semester. I was more nervous waiting to find out if he had been accepted than I was for myself back in high school. Finally the letter came and it became official: a fourth Gerhardt had become a Spartan. In my wildest dreams I had never imagined being a student on the same college campus as my brother. First of all, he graduated from high school three years before I did, and then went away to Kansas to start his college career. David's inability to pass physiology at KU resulted in one of the greatest experiences of my life, and would also bring about a new addition and relationship for my brother that nobody could have anticipated.

His first semester, it was nice to know he was around, but I hardly saw David on campus. It also meant I had another form of transportation other than the university and city bus system. My parents allowed my brother to have our family van, which was equipped with a wheelchair lift and lock-down system for my wheelchair. He also provided some relief to my health care provider, so he wasn't overwhelmed helping me out every morning and evening. It was working out great.

Since David enrolled so close to the start of the semester, he was very limited in his housing options. As luck would have it, a friend of mine, whom I had initially met as a freshman in the dorms and then had classes with, was doing an internship in Chicago that semester and was looking to sublease her room in a house off campus. I put the two in touch with each other, and not too long after, David signed on the dotted line. The house he ended up living in was occupied by four other girls, which was a totally new and unforgettable experience for him.

On a side note, another one of the girls living in the house, Jinny Crawford, also happened to be subleasing her room as she was studying abroad for the semester. David became friends with the girls in the house and, naturally, after Jinny returned from being abroad, he got to know her. In fact, he got to know her so well that the two began dating and are currently engaged to get married. Jinny and David live in Chicago where she is a special education teacher for Chicago Public Schools and David is a Show Manager for Corcoran Enterprises, Inc.

In order for me to graduate within four years at Michigan State, I needed to take two classes during the summer of 1999 on campus, before my senior year. David was also planning on taking a full load that summer. I was able to stay in the same dorm room that I lived in during the previous school year and would be staying in for the upcoming academic year. The way the rooms were situated in the residence hall was with two rooms joined together by a bathroom connecting them in the middle. The person living on the other side of the connecting bathroom, or sweetmate as they were called, wasn't staying on campus that summer. My brother's sublease was expiring, so he once again was looking for a place to stay. I put him in touch with the residence hall director who allowed David to stay in the room connected to mine with the agreement that he would work maintenance and security over the summer.

Now you have to realize the extent of knowledge when it comes to handiwork for all Gerhardt males throughout history is basically being able to screw in a light bulb and not a whole bunch more. Some Gerhardts would like to think they know more than they do, but the reality is we're not very handy. Luckily for David, his job consisted of repainting walls and scrubbing or sweeping floors. Security meant checking to make sure the main doors were locked at a certain time and others weren't propped open by some of the kids that were staying there during various summer camps. In other words, it was a pretty cushy job—not to mention that the room he was staying in was air-conditioned because the resident that lived in it during the regular academic year had respiratory issues, so he needed one for his health.

It was also the first time David became my main health care provider. Growing up, there hadn't been much need for him to assist me with daily health care tasks. It wasn't until after he moved away and was at KU that I broke my leg and began using a wheelchair and required much more physical assistance. Even then, when he came back home to visit, my parents were the ones who helped me out. Initially, I actually felt a little awkward having him help me.

I have always hesitated to fully disclose to those closest to me some of the things I am not physically able to do; this would include my brother. My parents are the exception to this rule, for the most part, as I am around them so frequently it would be impossible to hide certain weaknesses or needs. I have always lived my life with the desire and drive to do anything and everything physically possible. The last thing I want is to have people feel sorry, pity, or treat me as an invalid. I know my friends and family would never do this, but I guess by trying to hide or not disclose some of my weaknesses, I'm subconsciously trying to protect the emotions of those closest to me. It's as if I place a direct relationship between my needs and the emotions of family and friends. As my needs increase, the emotions of others intensify. I never hesitate to ask for help in fear of somebody saying no. If I hesitate, it's due to wanting to prove to myself I can do something or because I'm still in the mode of trying to protect somebody else's emotions. I don't know, but maybe it's me not being ready to fully accept the continuous process of muscle deterioration that inevitably occurs with having a terminal disease. I'm sure a psychiatrist would have a field day with that one! Anyway, the toughest part for me was knowing my brother was going to see first-hand the basic needs I had every morning and night just to get through a day. Right or wrong, I didn't want David to have to fully comprehend or have the added stress of knowing how much this disease had made simple tasks such as washing my hair or tying my shoes impossible for me to do on my own.

Either David was a quick learner, or he pretty much knew all of the things I couldn't do on my own. It would be naïve of me to believe that as my brother he wasn't aware of these needs. I always find it interesting to see how people physically handle or move me around when caring for me. At first people are generally nervous that they are going to do something to hurt me and move me around as if I'm a china doll. As time goes by, they learn which body parts are more flexible than others and which movements can be done quicker than others. After getting into a routine, suddenly I get handled like a rag doll instead of a china doll, except from my brother. After years of transfers, changing clothes, showering, etc., he still handles me like a carton of eggs.

I was very lucky to have David living by me that summer, as he was just next door. As fate would have it, I would need to use our van and be driven to the hospital one night. Earlier in the day, I had been at one of my classes when all of a sudden I broke out in an excessive sweat and felt really nauseated. I left my class and went into the nearest restroom. I splashed some cold water on my face and hovered over the sink. The pain was rapidly increasing to where it literally felt as if somebody had grabbed my testicles, twisted them, and then squeezed some more. I don't know how to put into words for females what that feels like, but I can just see the anguish in every male's face! After regaining my composure, I went back to my dorm room and fortunately my brother was there. I had him transfer me onto the toilet in hopes that would help my cause; it didn't. David had a class he needed to go to, so I had him help me into bed so I could try to rest and maybe sleep off the pain. He said he'd be back as soon as his class was over to check on me. The first thirty minutes he was gone was the closest I have ever come to calling an ambulance on my own. It was literally all I could do not to scream in pain. Then all of a sudden, like the flip of a switch, the pain was gone, and I was able to go to sleep. When David got back, I was still feeling fine and had him help me back into my chair. The rest of the day passed with no pain, so I wrote it off to some bad food or something to that effect.

Late that night I woke up with the same symptoms I had felt while in class. I knew at that point something was wrong, so I had David take me to the emergency room. They took me right in as they saw the major pain I was experiencing. After all kinds of tests, it was determined I had not one, but two kidney stones.

One of the side effects of taking my prednisone medication is it weakens bones. To counteract that, I took calcium supplements. Unfortunately, I was taking so much calcium that I developed the kidney stones, which are basically crystallized deposits of calcium that develop in the kidney and travel down the ureter to the bladder and eventually out through the urethra. Due to the location of the stones, the doctor recommended that I pass the stones naturally. Being that it was my first case of kidney stones, I wasn't aware of other ways to rid myself of them, so I took his advice of drinking tons of water, filled the prescription of pain medicine given to me, and went on my way.

The next week ended up being pure Hell. Having kidney stones in itself isn't painful; it's only when they move or travel inside of you that you then experience extreme pain. There is no way to prepare or tell when a stone is going to move. You can be feeling fine one moment, and then the next you're doubled over in the fetal position. I ended up going home for the week and even ended up making another trip to the emergency room one night in Traverse City for a shot of morphine. One of the female nurses on duty said that she had passed a kidney stone before and also had given child birth. She said she would rather go through child birth than have to pass another stone; that's how painful they can be.

After having the stones pass through my urethra, which is a sensation I can't even begin to describe, my parents took me back down to Michigan State. The first thing I noticed when I got into my room was both of my goldfish floating upside down in their bowl. Now normally this wouldn't be a huge thing, as goldfish are about a dime a dozen, but it was just one more addition to the week that was just about to get even worse.

I went to go check my answering machine, which seemed to have an alarming high number of messages compared to what would be normal for me. I couldn't believe what I was hearing. The majority of them were to inform me that my mentor and very close friend at MSU had died. Marge Chmielewski was the director of the Office of Programs for Handicapper Students. I first met Marge when I was a junior in high school while making a campus visit to MSU. From the first time I met her, she instilled a sense of confidence in me and assured my parents that MSU was a place where my needs would be taken care of. After enrolling in classes and arriving on campus, Marge became the first person I would go to should I have any problem—not just disability related, but anything and everything. Not only was she a mentor and resource, but she quickly became a friend and role model for me. Marge was a wheelchair user and had just completed her Ph.D. while holding down her director's position.

I knew she hadn't been feeling all that well over the last couple of months, but like me, she was never one to complain about or dwell on health issues. The last thing she would have wanted was for one of her students to be worried about her health issues. It turns out that a couple of weeks before I went into the emergency room for my kidney stones, she had been diagnosed with cancer. It had already traveled to her bones and was beyond the point of any treatment. The first message on my machine filled me in on her condition at that point and noted that I may want to go visit her in the hospital as time was running out. There were a few more messages from callers stating that they hoped they had my correct contact information since I hadn't returned any calls. Then the dreaded message came saying that Marge had passed away, along with the funeral arrangements. Not only had I missed seeing her one last time, I also had missed the funeral. It's amazing what can happen in just one week.

Although that was definitely the low point of the summer, being able to be with my brother with such intimate responsibilities really took our relationship to another level. I don't think people realize how important their role as a health care attendant is until it dawns on them what would happen if they didn't show up. It's not like I can struggle and eventually get myself up and ready. If my attendant doesn't show up, I'm stuck practically in the exact spot and position they left me the night before, or I'm in my chair if they don't show up at night. There is an inevitable trust and bond that develops when things run smoothly.

Even though over the previous few years our relationship as brothers had developed into more of a friendship, by having David as my care giver, it materialized into something greater. I was able to open up and let him see and be a part of my life that I had previously tried to shield from him. In return, through his care and reliability, David let me know he would always be there for me, not because he had to, but because he wanted to. I will always remember and cherish that summer we spent together as brothers, care giver and receiver, and college friends.

I don't know if David will ever fully comprehend how much he means to me. He says the same things about me, so maybe he does know how I feel. I'm so proud of everything he has accomplished, and I know I wouldn't be the person I am today without his example. He is a quiet leader and chooses to do more by actions than with words. I know he's shared through my parents some of the guilt he's felt at times when I've been in the hospital for either muscular dystrophy or non-MD related stays. As natural as it is for me to wonder at times, "why me?" it's just as normal for him to ask of himself, "why NOT me?" The answer to that question is simple for me. No matter how many trips to the hospital I encounter, I'd never pass one off to a loved one just to subtract one from my running total.

I've learned lots of lessons from multiple people during my life and look up to many others. I've also had the opportunity to meet some famous people in various professions. Through all of that, I truly have only one hero in my life. Not only is David my big brother, he's one of my best friends and my hero.

CHAPTER 12

O THER THAN fracturing my femur while in high school, which obviously was a huge incident, I had never really experienced any major injury or trauma aside from my muscular dystrophy diagnosis. I remember as a child joking with my mom that other than my MD, I was perfectly healthy! That perfect track record drastically changed in the fall of 2001.

Where were you when the date 9/11 changed from just another day on the calendar to a tragic event to forever be included in history books? On the night of September 9, 2001, I was playing in a non-competitive scrimmage of wheelchair (floor) hockey with a group of players from a league I was in. This was the very last get-together before the regular season was to start for my first full season as a league member on a team. Don't ask me why, but for some reason I didn't have my seatbelt fastened while we were playing: Mistake Number 1. There was a bunching up of most of the players fighting for the ball in the corner when it somehow popped out and was headed down towards the goal my team was attacking. I broke free and thought I was on my way for an uncontested breakaway: Mistake Number 2. There was still one defender who was able to angle himself and close in on the ball from the opposite direction. I could tell I would get to the ball before he would, even if it was just an instant beforehand. I figured he'd tail off and just try to cut my angle to the goal, as opposed to going for the ball: Mistake Number 3. We collided in what remained my biggest collision, and I ended up doing my best Superman impersonation.

Unfortunately, I landed on the floor in a butterfly or face-first snow-angel position with my hip flexors adducting. I remember lying on the floor and telling everybody that had rushed out to help me to just let me lie there for a minute to collect myself and try to move as many parts of my body as possible to see if there were any quick obvious pains or injuries. With no pains resembling my fractured femur experience, I had a couple of the dads turn me over, and told them to try to manipulate and move my legs.

Upon impact with the floor, I felt what I described as a tearing sensation up towards my left quad muscle or hip area. Everything seemed to be all right everywhere else, but I knew I had done something to that spot. I had full flexion and extension with my left leg, but external rotation caused me to yell. There was a doctor on site, and we felt there wasn't a fracture, due to the amount of movement I was able to tolerate—once again, not the last time my ability to tolerate a high level of pain would mask a more serious injury.

After being picked up and placed back in my chair, I rested on the sideline for a while and tried to relax. That got boring, so after a while, I went back in and played a little more. OK, I admit I went back in and just played goalie, but nonetheless, nobody could accuse me of being soft.

After driving myself back home, which takes about an hour, I was in more pain and decided to ice down the area; that seemed to help a little bit, but I knew I was in for a challenge, as I still had to get transferred out of my chair over to the toilet and change out of my pants for the night. Eric, my aide, helped me over to the toilet, and from my reaction he knew in his head it was more than just a muscle tear which I had described. I broke out into an intense sweat, and my throat got instantly dry; he said that I turned ghostly white.

Having a disability, you learn to throw out your modesty at an early age; but with all of the aspects of my life I needed assistance with, I still took pride in that I was able to handle all of my toileting and aspects of my personal hygiene. In a blink of an eye, this had all suddenly changed. It physically hurt too much to lean forward in order to wipe my butt. There I sat on the toilet, making sure I wasn't going to pass out from the transfer, in pain from trying to come up with any angle possible in order to wipe myself, knowing what I was going to have to ask.

I called for Eric to come in for what he thought was a continuation of our routine as he had a clean shirt and boxers for me to change into for bed. Before he could start to slide my new boxers on, I informed him there was a slight change of plans! He handled the news with so much class and allowed me to maintain my dignity. I'll never forget that situation and always will be so thankful for his attitude. We were even able to joke about it as he stated, "I can honestly say, I never imagined allowing my hand to do this on purpose!" Sometimes all you can do is laugh.

After struggling to get back in my wheelchair, we decided a trip to the emergency room was in my best interest. I must have been in the waiting room for what seemed like a couple of hours—too bad it wasn't the longest in my life that I'd have to wait to be seen at a hospital for x-rays on a possible fracture.

Even with the considerable amount of pain I was in, I didn't feel as if I had broken a bone. I still had vivid memories from when I had fractured my femur in high school and this was nothing like that. As soon as the doctor walked through the curtain in my emergency room space, I could tell from her expression that it wasn't good news. She said I had fractured my greater trochanter. First of all, I didn't even know what that was, and second, a fracture? I was in shock and disbelief. All I could think about was having to go through another surgery and the long rehab process I was in for. The doctor explained that the greater trochanter is the protrusion on the outside of the shaft of the femur at which point the thigh and hip muscles attach. When I fell, the stress from the impact of the floor and stretch on the muscle basically caused it to pull so much that it ripped from the bone and caused the fracture.

In my head, I was starting to compile a list of all the people I would immediately need to talk to and assist in my action plan. The doctor was talking about all kinds of things, but they were going in one ear and out the other until I heard four words that had to be mistaken. She said, "You won't need surgery." She added, "With this type of fracture, you can either let it heal on its own or be placed in a full body cast." The second option didn't sound too inviting, so I inquired more about letting it heal on its own. My using a wheelchair would actually benefit the healing process, as the chair would act as a splint during the day.

After leaving the hospital with one hand full of prescriptions for pain pills and the other full of bills, Eric and I made our way back to the apartment. It was now around 3 A.M. on Sunday, September 10. I knew I had to call my parents to inform them of everything. Any call at that time of the night can only be bad news, so I tried my best to explain the situation to them as calmly as possible to emphasize I was going to be all right. With the time of the call and all things considered, they took the news quite well. They both made lesson plans for their classes for Monday and Tuesday, and then made the three-hour trip down to East Lansing from Traverse City.

Trying to sleep was rough that Sunday night. I got up early Monday morning, and it was then that I got a phone call from a friend saying, "You might want to turn the TV on and check out the news." With my leg propped up in front of me, I sat there with my parents in disbelief as the Twin Towers in New York City came crumbling down before our very own eyes.

That's where I was on the morning of 9/11.

CHAPTER 13

EVERYBODY HAS one; even if you don't own one, you still have one. Everybody has a dog story. Mine just has an especially special element to it.

Ted and I became a pair in November of 2001. I had been apprehensive about the idea of getting a service dog, but my parents were excited about the whole concept. It's not that I don't like dogs; I love dogs. My family had a total of four different Airedales at one point or another as I was growing up.

They say you are either a dog or a cat person, and I'm definitely on the dog side, but I wasn't sure I wanted or could even handle the responsibility that went along with being a dog owner. For the first time I was living off campus in an apartment with three other friends. I had completed my bachelor's degree and was in the second year of my graduate program. I also was completing an internship with the Michigan High School Athletic Association, conveniently located in East Lansing. I had gotten used to having somebody other than my parents take care of my health care needs and was living as independently as I ever had. I saw a service dog as providing assistance that I really didn't need. Everybody else seemed more thrilled for me and convinced that this was going to make my life so much easier.

The letter came about a month before the training was to begin. I would have to go to Delaware, Ohio, along with one other person to receive the training and be paired up with a specific dog. My dad made the trip with me and, quite honestly, it was an experience neither of us will ever forget.

Some agencies simply have people fill out a brief questionnaire or form and then pair the person with a service dog, based off those few questions and medical reports. Canine Companions for Independence (CCI) has a more in-depth process. I had to get letters from friends, write an essay on how I felt a service dog would be an asset for me, complete a written application, and have an in-person interview. This was all done so that their trainers could get to know my personality, daily living habits and abilities in order to pair me with what they felt was the best trained dog they had available.

At CCI, puppies begin their journey in the homes of volunteer breeders where the parent dogs also live. When the puppies are two months old, they are brought to the Santa Rosa, California, facility that houses full-time veterinary and kennel care staffs. Following examination and vaccination, the puppies are placed in the homes of volunteer puppy raisers through one of CCI's five regional centers. The dogs are returned to their regional centers at approximately 14 months old and begin a six—to nine-month program of Advanced Training. They are fully trained and then introduced to the people who may become their partners during Team Training, which lasts two full weeks. At the end of the training, a public graduation ceremony takes place, marking the beginning of a long-term relationship between the recipient and dog and between the team and CCI.

At Team Training, there are actually more dogs than possible recipients. The first few days people are matched with different dogs while trainers observe the interaction and relationships between them. There were approximately ten of us in my class. We were all told on the first day not to get attached to any dogs, as CCI would have the final say in the pairings. CCI uses Golden Retrievers, Labrador Retrievers, and crosses of these two breeds. I've always had a preference for Black Labs over Golden or Yellow Labradors and was hopeful going into training that I would be so paired. When we were introduced to all the possible dogs, I was disappointed to see only two Black Labs out of all the possible dogs. I later found out they were actually Golden Retriever/Black Lab crosses and were brothers. Even though we had been specifically told not to get our hearts set on a specific dog, mine had already sold.

In order for consistent training to take place, breeders are allowed to name the puppies, and these names must be kept by recipients. Although it is a name I would never have given to a dog, it is a name that totally fit his personality. If there was ever a dog that matched the name Ted, this one fit that mold. The very first time we were matched up to work together, I knew there was a special relationship. Ted immediately jumped up, placing his front two paws on my lap, and lunged forward in an attempt to start kissing my face! Obviously this was not proper CCI protocol and could have been a major black mark on our performance in the eyes of the trainers, particularly if I didn't respond enthusiastically. Rather than immediately pushing Ted off my lap and disciplining him, I started to laugh and talk to him in the way that people do in high-pitched voices to dogs or babies. Needless to say, I received a brief lecture on how to properly handle "excitable greetings". Nevertheless, a bond had been created that I was going to do everything within my power to cement.

Over the course of the next few days, I primarily worked in a rotation with three different dogs. Luckily, Ted was still in that rotation. Other than our first welcome kiss, I felt Ted and I had become very consistent, and I couldn't help but to start to feel connected to him. I can admit it now that I actually started to mess up intentionally with the other dogs I was working with, just to make it appear that a match with Ted would work even better for me.

The first week of Team Training was coming to an end and we reached the day where partnerships would be assigned. We were all brought into the large training room where all the dogs were lying down together. It was an unbelievable site to see these ten dogs, all in their blue CCI working vests, just lying down as calm as could be, as ten wheelchair users entered the room about to receive the news that would change both humans' and dogs' lives more than anyone could ever anticipate.

I quickly noticed that a few of the dogs that had been in the training sessions were missing, as the number of wheelchair users and dogs was then equal. This wasn't the end of the road for these dogs; they would get another chance to be paired up during the next Team Training session scheduled a few months down the road. We all made a big circle around the dogs and one-by-one a trainer would go and pick up the leash to one of the dogs and slowly walk over and hand off the dog to a recipient, sometimes changing directions at the last minute only to intensify the suspense that had accumulated.

I had been watching Ted with others throughout the week and had basically come to the conclusion that there was one other person in the group that I was up against. There was also one other dog that I had been working well with, and I was trying to convince myself to be happy should this pairing be made. She ended up being placed next, which still left me without a leash in my hand. That narrowed the field to four dogs, Ted being one of those, and four wheelchair users, one of whom I knew was the other strong possibility for Ted. The next dog, not being Ted, went to him, and I felt as if all that remained was the formality of Ted being walked over to me. We celebrated our pairing by doing a "lap" command and finishing it off with a kiss, the same way we greeted each other for the first time earlier in the week!

After two weeks of intensive training, all of a sudden I was leaving Ohio and heading back to my graduate classes at Michigan State with a dog that was supposed to make my life much easier. Or at least that's what all of my friends and family had been telling me over and over again. Little did I realize at the time what changes this canine would bring into my life.

When I got back to my apartment and said good-bye to my parents, the reality of the situation hit me. Yes, I had a service dog that was going to help me out, but I also had a dog that needed to be fed, taken to the bathroom, groomed, and exercised daily. I'm not even able to take care of myself without the assistance of my home help care provider. How was I supposed to take care of the needs of my dog? After being in a power wheelchair for over six years, I had become a master at maneuvering tight corners and making my way through cramped aisles. Now, all of a sudden, I was going to have to get through those tight spaces with a dog by my side, not to mention a tail that always seemed to be wagging out of control in excitement. My hand that didn't control my wheelchair, and was free to open doors, now had a leash in it. Winter was quickly approaching, which meant I would be having to go outside in the cold Michigan snow multiple times each day—a task challenging enough just on my own—for

Ted to do his business. This dog was supposed to make my life easier and give me more independence. After all, it was right there in the name of the organization, Canine Companions for *Independence*. Instead, it seemed as if things had just become a lot more strenuous for me, and I'd be depending on people even more.

What had I gotten myself into? Why couldn't I have been placed with Ted when I was younger and still living at home with my parents, where they could have helped me take care of all of Ted's needs? Of course, at that time in my childhood, I wasn't ready emotionally to accept a service dog. I still needed to prove to myself that I could do things on my own and would be able to someday live away from my parents and go to college. Now I was ready emotionally, having already proved to myself all I needed, but physically the responsibilities were overwhelming.

I've never had a problem asking for help when I've needed it. I've always lived under the notion that there are far more nice people in this world than not, and they will go out of their way to assist when asked. This situation was different for me though. Being born with a neuromuscular disease wasn't something I, or anybody else, asked for. It's just been a part of my everyday life, and I deal with it the best way that I know how. Having a service dog was a choice; I didn't have to have one. How was I supposed to ask for all of this help from my roommates and friends when these were responsibilities that I should be taking care of on my own? On top of that, I wouldn't be asking for help with fun stuff. The same people I was telling not to pet my service dog because he was working, I was going to have to ask to help with taking him outside and picking up after he went to the bathroom. It didn't exactly seem like a fair trade, coming from their perspective.

Why hadn't I thought of all the responsibilities beforehand? I had grown up in a family that had dogs and had seen all the time and patience they took. Why hadn't my parents made me think about all of these things previously? Wait a minute . . . wasn't it their idea in the first place that I should get a service dog? Weren't they the ones who convinced me this would be a good thing? Maybe they had, but the final decision had ultimately been mine. There was no way I could turn back at this point.

Actually, that wasn't totally true. I could have turned back—and almost did. I could have returned Ted to CCI and said the responsibility was too much for me because I couldn't take care of Ted's daily needs. It would have been a tough and very emotional decision, but one that I still could have made.

The short amount of time it took to become emotionally attached to Ted, however, was amazing to me. Even though I was having all of these doubts about my ability to keep him, already I couldn't imagine my life without my new buddy. There's a good reason why dogs are known as man's best friend.

It's hard for me to believe that Ted and I have been a team for seven years. We have our rituals, can maneuver tight corners, and are able to make it through aisles without Ted's tail knocking everything over. Yes, I still need help feeding, grooming, and picking up after him. Yes, honestly sometimes I still do struggle asking for help with these chores. I try to do as much as I can in helping with Ted's needs, not because I have to, but because I want to in return for all that he does for me. It's hard for me to imagine my life without Ted, and it's something that gets me very emotional when I think about it. Everywhere we go he automatically becomes the center of attention. People still come up to me on a regular basis and say, "I bet he has made things so much easier for you." Rather than getting into a long conversation, I usually just smile really big and

respond by saying something to the effect of, "He sure is an amazing and wonderful friend," and I give Ted a scratch behind his ears.

My friends ask me if I will get another service dog after Ted. I honestly don't know and probably won't be able to answer that question until the time comes. My first inclination is to say "no" for a couple of reasons. As all dog lovers can attest, I can't imagine another dog being able to replace Ted. It says a lot that when writing this book, the only chapter where my eyes started to fill with tears was when I started to think of my life without Ted. Disease, broken heart, blindness, accidents, injuries, human death—they didn't do it, but thinking of his death or having to put my dog to sleep, that makes me emotional! He's more than just a dog; he's a member of my family. Second, I'm not sure I can commit to all that goes into maintaining a dog, of any kind, on my own. Now should I be married and have children of my own, that is a whole different story.

The best part of Ted is his unconditional love. He knows that I am different and that I use a wheelchair. He walks right next to me up against my wheelchair, yet knows not to get too close or he'll get his paws rolled over. He knows without me even having to give him the command, to pick up objects should I drop them. Yes, I'm different, but to Ted that is a good thing. Other people don't require any assistance from him. He is actually happiest when doing something for me. I can see it in his eyes and mannerisms. Sometimes when I'm alone I'll drop something on purpose just so that he can assist me and so I can praise him for helping. He knows I'm different, but to Ted different is better.

Truth be told, no, Ted has not made life easier for me, but one thing is for sure; Ted sure has made life better for me. Maybe I was looking at CCI's name all wrong. I should have seen it as Canine *Companions* for Independence!

CHAPTER 14

ANOTHER ONE of the problems or side-effects of being on prednisone for a prolonged period of time is that it causes bruising and poor circulation. These problems are compounded by the fact that I'm sitting in a wheelchair all day long. You'd be amazed at how much your body benefits from just being able to stand up and walk around during the normal routine of a day, not to mention the calories you burn.

It was one of the last weekends in August of 2002, and I was at my parent's house packing to get ready to go on one of my first extended road trips. It was an end of the summer trip I had planned for some time where I was going to visit and stay with Kevin, who was in Madison, Wisconsin.

There had been a big thunderstorm earlier in the day, so my dad had unplugged all the cords from his computer. He always struggled reconnecting to the Internet correctly, so that night he called me in to the computer room to help him make sure everything was done correctly. Neither one of my parents is great when it comes to understanding the latest advancements in technology. They also both hate reading instructions or following manuals, which just compounds the issue.

I had just gotten out of the shower, and normally after getting dried off, I would get back into my wheelchair and then just head into my bedroom and get put into bed. My bedroom is directly across the hall from the bathroom, so I never would bother putting my footrests back on my wheelchair because they would just have to come right back off in ten seconds. So, as the normal routine called for, I didn't have my footrests on; but instead of heading straight for my room, I went one room further down the hall to where the computer was located.

We didn't have a traditional computer desk, so instead we used a portable counter-top placed on two heavy-duty metal filing cabinets at each end to support it. I pulled up to where I could still see under the counter top and the various cords hanging down, but still left enough room so my dad could crawl underneath and make the necessary connections based on my directions.

As my dad started to bend over, the sleeve on his t-shirt accidentally hooked over the joystick control on my wheelchair, which I hadn't turned off yet, and sent me accelerating forward. Without the footrests on my chair, there was nothing to protect my legs as I went crashing into one of the filing cabinets. My left shin slammed into the corner of one of the cabinets, causing it to slice open while my right shin collided with the metal handle that was protruding out of the front of it.

We both knew the situation wasn't a good one as instantly blood literally shot out from my leg and was all over the place. Immediately my dad got some clean rags and wrapped them around the bleeding area and elevated my leg. With my mom holding the rags in place and my dad driving, we made a late-night trip to the emergency room.

Luckily it didn't take too long to get called back and to be seen by a doctor. I explained to him what had happened, and then he slowly started to remove the bloody rags that were wrapped around the wound. Once he saw my leg for the first time, I think he was taken aback at how severe the cut was. I'm sure in his head he had envisioned a simple stitch job and that I'd soon be on my way back home. Not so fast; this would be more than just a simple stitch job.

The integrity of the skin on my legs is also very poor and thin. The attempts to stitch the skin back together were useless because the needle simply tore through the remaining skin. After a couple of failed attempts, the emergency room doctor decided that the situation was too complex for him to handle. He ended up laying as much of the torn skin as possible back in place and wrapping the wound in new sterile bandages, and I was referred to a plastic surgeon. This all occurred on Friday night, so of course I wasn't able to meet with the new doctor until the following Monday. I was instructed to keep my leg elevated all weekend long and limit its movement as much as possible. So much for my first road trip!

Monday finally came, and I was able to meet with the plastic surgeon, Dr. Smith. He recognized the complexity of my case and wanted to do everything possible in order to prevent a possible surgery. Stitches obviously would not work, so we began a process of trying to heal the wound from the inside out with advanced topical gels. He said that it would be a very slow and long treatment, but one that had proven successful in similar cases. The process involved applying a precise amount of a prescribed gel onto the wound every night, after cleaning it out with the proper solution, and then covering and wrapping it with sterilized bandages. After about a week of doing this, I ran into my first complication: the bruise on the right leg from banging into the handle on the filing cabinet had opened

up and was oozing all kinds of gunk. I was able to get in to see Dr. Smith right away, and he recommended we start the same treatment on it.

Let me also add that this was not a comfortable treatment. Applying the gel itself didn't burn or anything like that; the pain was due more to the wounds being open to the level of my nerve endings. So to put the gel on, pressure was applied directly to exposed nerves.

Slowly, progress could be seen, and it appeared as if I would be able to avoid having any type of surgery. The wounds were clearing up and appeared to be filling in more and more from the inside out. Interestingly, the bruise that had opened up after the injury was healing less well than the cut on my opposite shin. After approximately three months, the gash on my left shin had completely filled in and could be deemed as fully healed. I still have one heck of a scar as a reminder, but the treatment had served itself well. Unfortunately, the same couldn't be said for my right shin. Initially it seemed as if the process was working, but the healing seemed to have plateaued and the opening was still oozing various fluids. There were no signs of infection, so we decided to keep with the same plan of treatment for another month to see if there would be any noticeable improvements.

Another month went by and nothing improved. It was then that Dr. Smith and I came to the conclusion that I was down to my final option of having surgery to physically close the wound. Leaving it as it was would be too risky because of the possibility of infection developing, or even worse, traveling to the bone.

Dr. Smith explained he would perform a skin graft where he would take some of my own skin from inside my thigh, about two-by-four inches, and place it over the wound where it would grow and attach to the existing skin around the current wound. He showed me some of the tools he would be using, which seemed to me to resemble a cheese slicer which would peel off a layer of skin. It's a delicate process and one that would require a hospital stay following surgery. When the skin is attached to the wound, there needs to be as little movement as possible so the skin doesn't wrinkle or move around. I would have to remain in the hospital for about a week to keep my lower leg elevated and in a splint. This was a little longer than most other patients with the same procedure, but necessary because I wouldn't be able to move myself around without the assistance of others, and would need greater health care.

Speaking with Dr. Smith following surgery, he felt everything went well; and it was a good thing we hadn't waited any longer, because the wound was starting to travel deeper and would have eventually gotten to the bone. There was plenty of dead blood in the area, along with other fluids that had prevented healing, due to the deepness and severity of the bruise.

I was amazed at how much better the area on my shin felt almost instantly following surgery, at least in a resting position. Any movement resulting in a change of height caused major throbbing, but that was all right since I wasn't supposed to be moving it at that point. Dr. Smith explained the lack of pain was because for the first time in months, my nerve endings weren't exposed. Sure, there was the trauma from the surgery, but everything was covered up and back in working order. As far as where the skin had been taken from inside my thigh, that was a different story!

Now you have to understand that they don't remove every layer of skin from the donor site; that of course would leave a huge hole. As I explained before, they delicately remove enough layers so they can be placed over a wound, attach, grow, and eventually form to the area and act like the initial skin. The best way to describe the donor site is to compare it to a deep severe burn. I would have to say the pain or discomfort from the donor site was ten times worse than the post-surgery discomfort around the initial wound area. It's something all skin graft patients have to go through, but that doesn't make it any less painful.

After being discharged from the hospital, I went back to my parents' house. I still had to have my leg elevated and was only allowed to have it down for a period of up to half an hour a few times during the day for the first few days. After that, I was allowed to gradually build up the length and frequency until after a few weeks I could have it down as much as I could tolerate. Luckily, I still had the leg-extender for my wheelchair that I had used after fracturing my leg in high school, so I was able to use my wheelchair and get around without any added assistance.

It took about one full month until I was ready and able to return to my apartment and move back away from my parents. It was close to six months post-surgery that I wasn't in any discomfort at either the initial wound or donor site. After close to one year following the accident, Dr. Smith discharged me and I was done supporting all of those who had stock in gauze and medical tape, or at least so I thought.

CHAPTER 15

As MUCH as I liked Dr. Smith, I had hoped to not have to see him again or at least under similar circumstances. However, almost exactly one year after being involved in the accident with my dad, it was time for my mom to enter the picture.

She was visiting my apartment and had given my health care attendant the morning off by helping me on her own. For some reason, that morning I was feeling a little under the weather, so I asked my mom to help me to the toilet. Normally I just use a urinal in the mornings and don't actually sit on the toilet until the evenings. She transferred me from my bed to my wheelchair and then, once in my bathroom, over to the toilet.

This all went smoothly, and I was actually feeling a little better after doing my business. I called my mom back into the bathroom; and after getting my boxers pulled back up, we started with our transfer from the toilet back to my wheelchair. Normally, when I'd be doing this transfer, it would be at night and I would still be wearing a pair of socks. You'd think this would make the transfer more difficult, but it actually made things easier, as the socks would allow me to basically slide with the assistance of the lifter, as opposed to having my feet stick on the bathroom floor.

Being that this was the morning as opposed to the night routine, things were a little out of order. I didn't have socks on yet, and as luck would have it, after pivoting to turn from the toilet and sit in my wheelchair, my right foot got caught behind one of the front tires. This in itself was somewhat uncomfortable, but wouldn't have caused any damage had it not been that there just happened to be a loose screw extending out from its slot in the hub of that same front tire. Needless to say, that screw punctured right through my skin just above my ankle and tore a nice new deep wound about the size of a quarter. Once again, blood was all over the floor, and I was in a great deal of pain. I still had plenty of bandages from my previous wounds and skin graft, so after carefully describing to my mom which way to move my foot so it would not only get uncaught behind the wheel, but also unhooked from the screw, we quickly got this one wrapped up.

Just getting me bandaged up was traumatic enough for my mom, but now she needed to get me to the emergency room. That doesn't seem like that big of a deal, except you have to realize she had driven down to see me in her SUV, not the family van which has a wheelchair lift on it. The only available accessible vehicle was the mini-van I drive with hand-controls, which she had never driven before. The hand-controls can be deactivated, and it can be driven using the regular factory controls, but lots of the adaptive controls for features such as the turn signals, headlights, windshield wipers, etc. are still active. The buttons for these are located where I rest my left forearm by the driver's door, so it is very easy for an able-bodied driver to bump and activate these features on accident or without realizing what is happening.

I also drive from my wheelchair, so the driver's seat has been pulled out. In order for somebody else to drive, the front passenger's seat gets popped out and placed in the driver's side. My wheelchair then fits in the passenger's side. After instructing my mom how to move the seat over to the driver's side so she had something to sit on, we were on our way. The expression and coloring on her face was all I needed to see in order to know that just getting to the emergency room would be an adventure. My mom is usually great in high pressure situations, but I could tell she was really shaken. I slowly talked her through some of the basics of the adaptive features, and we were on our way.

She quickly got to know the buttons for the adaptive features, and before you knew it, we had the windshield wipers going on this glorious, hot, sunny morning. I tried to explain to her, as she was driving, how to turn the wipers back off, but all this did was activate the horn and turn the front defroster on. So now we've got other drivers staring at us as we're going down the street with our windshield wipers activated and horn going on and off. Meanwhile, we were already hot and sweaty enough from the stress of the situation, but then she has the heater going full blast. This all would have been very comical had it not been that my ankle was completely gashed open, and in my head I was already figuring out how much time this would set me back. Before we passed out from overheating, I was able to instruct her to turn the defroster off and also got the wipers turned off. Somehow through that process, she activated the hazard blinkers. I figured this was actually a good thing and told her to leave them on for the remainder of our memorable trek to the hospital.

Once inside the emergency room, I got admitted right away. As I explained to the doctor what had just happened, along with my history of non-healing wounds, we discussed our options. Because this wound was located just above my ankle and in a little more "meatier" area than my shin, the doctor wanted to attempt to stitch it up. Even if he couldn't get the stitches to hold, we wouldn't be in any worse situation than where we were at the moment. He used a couple of different methods where there was both internal and external stitching along with one continuous stitch. After over an hour's worth of work, he finally announced he was done and had successfully gotten everything to hold. The whole process required more than twenty stitches, but getting the stitches to hold was only half the battle. The doctor explained that just because the stitches were currently holding didn't mean they would continue to hold or the wound itself would close or seal.

Sure enough, a couple of days later the upper stitches split and the top part of the wound was open. I went back to see the doctor, and we were a little amazed at how strongly the stitches in the middle and the bottom were holding. We decided at that point to remove the top stitches which had split, but leave the remaining ones in hopes they would heal at least the lower portion of the opening.

The stitches ended up holding, but after two weeks they had to be removed in order to prevent any type of infection from setting in. Here was the big test; did the stitches do their job and had my skin healed enough to hold together except for the upper part, which then we'd concern ourselves with, or would we be back at square one and figure out a new path of healing? Square one it was.

Out came the stitches, and the wound opened right back up. Dr. Smith, here I come! Drastic situations call for drastic trials. This time around we had some prior history to draw on. Of course the history we were drawing upon had mixed results. The wound on my left shin, which was larger but shallower, eventually healed after using the topical gel method for two to three months. The same method didn't work on the right shin for the smaller, but deeper wound. My new wound was both large and deep, so it was either attempt something new or go straight to another skin graft. I was open to anything as long as it prevented my having to have another surgery and hospital stay.

The new brainstorm was something called Negative Pressure Wound Therapy (NPWT) using a vacuum-assisted closure (VAC) system. NPWT is a topical treatment intended to promote healing in acute and chronic wounds. It involves the application of negative pressure to the wound. The concept is to turn an open wound into a controlled, closed wound while removing excess fluid from the wound bed, improving circulation and disposal of cellular waste from the system. Negative pressure brings tissue together, encouraging the tissues to stick together through natural tissue adherence, which increases healing.

The VAC system is applied to an open wound for periods of 48 hours. Suction is directed at the surface of the wound through a sponge that is cut to the appropriate shape of the wound and is then inserted to contact the entire wound. The foam allows for distribution of the negative pressure. Suction tubing is placed in the foam, and then the entire wound is covered with a clear plastic dressing to seal it off. It is then connected to a portable suction pump for 48 hours per session, with either constant or intermittent suction. The drainage from the wound goes into a canister attached to the suction pump.

Making sure the sponge is cut to the exact size of the wound is vital, because it can irritate and infect or kill off the healthy skin located around the wound if the suction is applied to that area.

The concept for this treatment is a good one, but let me tell you something: it is extremely painful. Every aspect—applying it, utilizing it, removing it—hurts. The first couple of sessions weren't too bad, but once the wound started to heal and the sponge had to be placed over the exposed nerve endings, it nearly brought me to tears. The interesting thing when it comes to nerves is that the exact spot where they are exposed doesn't necessary correspond to the same location of pain. Every time suction was applied to the wound just above my ankle, I would receive a huge shooting pain across the top of my foot. It almost felt as if there was a broken bone in my foot and the slightest movement of my toes would only aggravate it more. I learned to deal with this and justified it with the hope that I was preventing a surgery.

After a month of treatments, it seemed like we were on the right path. The wound itself was extremely healthy and clean, at least according to the nurses who would change the sponges. To me it just looked like a patch of fried bologna. It had also decreased in size as the diameter was smaller and wasn't as deep. It had been a slow painful process, and I still had at least another month of treatments ahead of me.

The second month passed by, and my new measurements showed no new progress had been made. The wound was exactly the same size as a month earlier. After discussing things over with Dr. Smith, we decided to cut our losses and attempt another skin graft. My skin had proven that it would hold after my previous surgery was successful, so we would go through the same process.

This time surgery took place towards the middle of November, and I was released from the hospital the day before Thanksgiving. Even though the VAC didn't totally heal the wound, it made the surgery much easier, and there weren't any difficulties like the previous surgery when the trauma from the wound had almost traveled to the bone. The graft held with 100% coverage compared to roughly 85% on my shin, which still required some topical treatments post-surgery.

Once again, the pain from my ankle and foot seemed to be alleviated quickly, while the discomfort from the donor site was quite intense and lengthy.

It took about another full month until I didn't need to keep my foot elevated for some period of time and was able to once again move back on my own into my apartment. It was at that time I started wearing support hose daily over my lower legs. The hose do a couple of things for me as they have helped decrease the swelling or edema that pools in my lower legs from sitting in a wheelchair all day long, and they also act as another protective layer on top of my skin. As difficult as it is for my health care provider to put a pair of socks on me, just imagine how much harder it is to pull on a pair of hose that are more than twice as snug. It's worth the extra time and effort as my lower legs look and feel much better, and I haven't had any major traumas to them since that point in time.

CHAPTER 16

COME SUMMER of 2004, it appeared I had finally healed from all of my wounds and surgeries, so I had planned another trip to go visit Kevin and his girlfriend Emily in Wisconsin. This time I worked it out to go over the 4th of July weekend. The 4th fell on a Monday, so I had that day off from work, and I was also able to get the previous Friday off to make for a nice vacation. We made all kinds of plans beforehand for events that were going to be held over the holiday weekend; all of us had been looking forward to getting together for quite some time.

That Wednesday night I noticed my ankle was a little sore, like it was bruised. I pulled my sock down and noticed it was a little red, but nothing major. I figured I must have bumped it at some point during the day while in my wheelchair. I couldn't remember doing anything to it, but really didn't think too much about it.

Midway through the night, after going to bed, I woke up in a major sweat, and after wiggling around a little bit felt severe pain in my ankle. I have a hospital-style bed, so I sat myself up but still couldn't get the covers off enough to take a look at it. I called my roommate Eric in to help me, and after removing my covers, we were both shocked to see my ankle had ballooned to about twice the normal size and was quite red. All the signs pointed to another return visit to my friends at the Sparrow Hospital Emergency Room.

After the prerequisite lengthy wait, I was finally called back and eventually was able to be seen by a doctor. Of course, multiple blood and urine tests were done and ultimately it was declared that I had an infection in my ankle or more specifically a case of cellulitis.

Cellulitis is a potentially serious bacterial infection of the skin. It appears as a swollen, red area that feels hot and tender, and can spread rapidly. Skin on the face or lower legs is most commonly affected. Cellulitis may also affect the tissues underlying the skin and can spread to lymph nodes and the bloodstream. Left untreated, the spreading infection may result in amputation of the limb or rapidly turn into a life-threatening condition. That's why it's important to recognize the signs and symptoms early and to seek immediate medical attention if they occur. The only thing the doctors could trace the infection to was the skin graft surgery I'd had before the end of the previous year. Luckily, I caught it quickly enough ahead of time to where it was contained and didn't spread much further than my ankle. Unfortunately, it had gotten to the point where an oral antibiotic wouldn't have been strong enough, so I had to be admitted into the hospital and spent my 4th of July weekend stuck with my leg propped up in the air the whole time while receiving antibiotics intravenously.

Proving just how lucky I am to have such wonderful friends, Kevin and Emily decided to reverse plans and head over to East Lansing to visit me over the 4th of July, even though I was stuck in the hospital. I was shocked to see them, but it really lifted my spirits. They were only able to stay in town for one night and slept at my apartment even though I wasn't there. My parents had also come to town for the weekend so they were able to entertain a little in my place.

I wasn't on any type of food restrictions during my stay, so Saturday night they brought some take-out dinner to my room for all of us to eat together. Kevin and Emily also brought with them from Wisconsin something they called "squeaky cheese". More commonly it is known as Wisconsin curd cheese. When you bite down on it, it tends to squeak, hence the name. Anyway, I love just about all kinds of cheese, so I was up to trying a new kind.

I popped a piece in my mouth and was a little disappointed as it didn't seem to squeak as much as I had been anticipating. It tasted fine, nothing special, but better than your typical chunk of American cheese. What I did notice was that almost instantly after chewing on my piece, the sides of my mouth really started to tingle, and not in a good kind of way. It was as if I was being pricked by a bunch of tiny pins and needles on the insides of my cheeks. I was a little concerned, but tried not to think too much about it. I continued eating the rest of my food, but the tingling seemed to be getting worse, and it felt as if my tongue and cheeks were starting to swell. It got to the point where they felt large enough where I actually asked my friends and parents whether or not my face looked swollen. They said that it didn't, but at this point there was enough concern to where I called in my nurse. I explained the situation and decided I must have had an allergic reaction to the cheese. Before the swelling got any worse or traveled to my throat, the nurse decided to give me a dose of Benadryl through my IV. Almost instantly I could feel my tongue and cheeks reducing to normal size. The nurse must have given me a healthy dose because I started to feel a little dizzy and extremely tired. I was trying with all my might to keep my eyes open and be a good host, but it was a lost cause. Apparently my guests noticed my change and left so I could catch up on my sleep.

The next morning everybody stopped in and seemed to have their own stories on how I kept them entertained the previous night before I crashed and they left. I guess I was speaking a lot of nonsense, although since I didn't remember any of it, for all I know they could have been making things up right on the spot!

If that would have been my only medical setback in 2004, it would have been a decent year. The timing of it was disappointing in that once again it cancelled a trip I had planned to go and stay with Kevin in Wisconsin, but the overall severity wasn't too overwhelming. To this day, we still joke that I need to just jump in my car one weekend and head on out rather than planning well in advance and allowing the powers that be enough time to come up with a medical crisis prohibiting me from traveling.

Towards the middle of July, I noticed the vision in my right eye seemed to be a little more blurry than normal. I had known I had cataracts in both of my eyes, as a result from being on prednisone for a prolonged period, but neither one really affected my vision or progressed to the point where surgery was required. My optometrist had told me that I would be the one to know when surgery would be needed. If the cataract grew or moved in either eye, my vision would become blurry, and at that time we'd discuss surgery to remove it. I figured that's what had happened in my right eye, so I wasn't really scared and didn't feel the need to make an emergency appointment. I called my eye doctor and scheduled a time to see him a couple of weeks down the road.

The vision continued to get worse before my appointment; but once again, I just figured that was the progression of the cataract and it was time to have it removed. I met with my optometrist and explained the symptoms I'd been having. He too figured it was my cataract and performed a few tests.

That's when things started to take a turn for the worse. The cataract hadn't changed at all, so my doctor was worried it was something more. He referred me to an ophthalmologist, and he personally made a call to get me in that same day. That's when I knew we were dealing with something quite serious. If it had been something normal, there wouldn't have been the need to be seen right away.

I basically had time to go to my parents' house and eat lunch before heading back to meet with the new ophthalmologist. He apparently had been informed of my symptoms and started performing tests right away. It didn't take him long to find what he was looking for before he turned off all of his equipment, rolled a few feet back on his stool, took a deep breath through his nose and started his "I have some bad news . . ." speech.

I've heard a million of them from various doctors, so I knew what his body language was indicating. I just wasn't sure how bad *bad* was going to be. He explained that he felt I had a condition known as Central Retinal Vein Occlusion or CRVO. He couldn't be positive without using some specialized equipment, but all evidence led to that diagnosis. He said he wanted to refer me to a retina specialist in town who could make a definitive diagnosis and would be able to fill me in on all the details associated with the disorder. I still wasn't sure what this all meant for me as far as my vision was concerned, but figured I would save all my questions for the specialist I was about to go see.

It never ceases to amaze me how quickly things in life can change. At the beginning of the day, I was headed to my family eye doctor to see when I could have some outpatient eye surgery to remove what I thought was a problem with my cataract, and return to normal vision. A few hours later and now I'm headed to see my third doctor of the day and curious as to whether or not I was ever going to be able to recover any vision in my right eye at all.

Once again, I could tell this was serious, as I was admitted right away to see the specialist upon arriving at his office. He put more drops in my eyes, and at this point they felt like they were on fire from all the various solutions that had been placed in them. After a couple of bright lights and looking through various machines, he too did the traditional sit on the stool roll away from the patient move and took a deep breath. He confirmed what the previous doctor had suggested: I had a case of CRVO.

The doctor described Central Retinal Vein Occlusion as a complicated problem that can cause a significant loss of vision. One occurs when the blood flow out of the eye through the central vein becomes sluggish or completely obstructed. No one understands what causes the blood flow to slow. It is thought that somehow the central vein becomes clogged up inside or perhaps pinched by some structure from the outside.

Whatever the cause, the blood cannot get out of the eye, and it begins to back up, much like a stopped-up drain in a sink or a dam on a river. The blood vessels behind the obstruction—in this case the smaller veins feeding into the central vein—begin to swell with the extra blood. Soon the pressure in the veins begins to build, and blood begins to seep out of the veins and into the retina; this appears as bleeding in all areas of the retina. If the obstruction is severe enough, the pressure will drive more and more blood and fluid into the retina, causing it to swell like a sponge.

Generally, a central retinal vein occlusion is classified by its severity into one of two types. These two types are called by many different terms but can most easily be thought of as mild or severe. The mild form may also be called impending or non-ischemic vein occlusion, and the severe may be called complete or ischemic vein occlusion. As my luck would have it, I had the more severe ischemic form.

In the more severe form, the blood flow is completely obstructed. The blood may even back up so much that fresh blood cannot enter the retina through the arteries. The cells in the retina become starved for oxygen that is normally brought in by the blood.

If the ischemia or lack of oxygen is very severe, the eye may attempt to grow new blood vessels. Although this may seem like a helpful response, the process of new blood vessel growth can be very destructive to an eye. If these blood vessels grow out of the retina, they can lead to a loss of vision from severe bleeding or retinal detachment. If they grow onto the iris, they may cause an unusual form of glaucoma to develop. Glaucoma is a condition in which the pressure inside the eye rises to intolerable levels. Known as neovascular glaucoma, this disease is almost impossible to treat with drops or medication and can lead to total blindness or loss of the eye.

The doctor said that although the process of central retinal vein occlusion has been extensively studied, no one yet understands exactly what causes this problem. It is known that it usually occurs in adults over 55 years old, but it may occur in young adults as well, as was my case.

The most frustrating aspect of this condition is that there is no treatment for it. Many investigators have studied this problem and attempted treatments without success. Scientists have tried to thin the blood and improve the flow with various blood thinners such as aspirin, warfarom, and heparin. They have tried using the same clot-busting agents that are used successfully in heart attacks and strokes, such as TPA and streptokinase. They have tried to lower the pressure in the eye to dilate blood vessels and promote better flow. They have surgically tried to create alternative blood flow channels. None of these approaches has had any real success.

If I had one thing going for me, it was that I was young. The doctor said that for some reason in cases with younger people, over the course of time, the body may reopen the vein on its own. If it will do so, it may take anywhere from a few months to a year for the vein occlusion to completely resolve.

We decided to hold off on any type of radical procedure and hope for the best—that maybe over the next few months I would start to see some improvements. I was prescribed some eye drops and scheduled with appointments to see the doctor on a weekly basis.

A month went by and no progress had been made. In reality, my vision had even become worse. Unfortunately, I was starting to develop new blood vessels, a process known as retinal neovascularization.

Waiting and hoping for improvement was no longer an option. I needed to have laser surgery performed to basically zap the new blood vessels that had been forming. Left untreated, they would continue to grow, which would result in the retina detaching.

I had the outpatient procedure and was told to take it easy for the next couple of days. After being re-examined by the doctor, he was a little concerned even with the procedure my retina was still going to detach due to the trauma and scar tissue build up, which is quite common.

Unfortunately, I would have to wait a few weeks to determine this. Meanwhile, the pressure in my eye continued to increase almost daily. None of the drops prescribed seemed to be working anymore to lower the pressure and pain level. At this point, I was having headaches constantly. I was seeing my eye doctor each week, and he was eventually able to tell that my retina had in fact detached. I would have to have another surgery performed, this time more involved, than before.

My headaches were becoming so painful that they were affecting my ability to work. I wanted to have the surgery as soon as possible, but the doctor told me that unfortunately I had to wait for the trauma from the previous laser surgery to settle down and for the eyeball itself to stabilize before another surgery could be performed on it.

A month went by, and my eye was finally in a state where surgery could be performed to reattach my retina. The pressure in my eye had gotten so high that my headaches now felt as if somebody had literally cracked me on the side of my head with a baseball bat. Even if it meant not being able to see out of my eye again, I had never been so ready for a surgery just to relieve some pain. Well, that wish is exactly what I got.

The doctor was able to successfully reattach my retina and even removed the existing cataract that was in that eye during the surgery. Although I wasn't required to stay at the hospital, I had to remain in a face-down position for the next two days. I didn't have to stay in bed the whole time, but when I was out of bed and seated in my wheelchair, all I was allowed to do was look down at the ground.

Unfortunately, CRVO is a very frustrating problem and final vision is often not very good. The visual outcome is rarely improved by any treatment since there is no way to alter the natural progression of the vein occlusion itself. Going into the surgery, I was still able to see color, light, and detect large objects with that eye, although that ability was quickly deteriorating. Following surgery, my doctor explained that I would initially see only total darkness out of that eye. This is the case with any retinal surgery. If I were to see improvement, the vision would return from the bottom up, sort of like a curtain being raised.

In some ways, it is sort of ironic. The pressure in my eye had increased so much and was causing me so much pain that my doctor feared a third surgery might have been required to simply release some pressure and eliminate the pain from which I was suffering. Well, once my eye recovered from the entire trauma of the first two surgeries, the pressure actually decreased to below what is considered normal. If you look closely at my eyes, you can actually tell my right eyeball is now smaller than my left one. It appears to be sunken in a little more and also has a tendency to be bloodshot.

The good news is that this decreased pressure in my eye does not cause me any pain or discomfort, and I no longer have any headaches due to the disorder.

Although there were a couple of times I thought I saw some light being shown at the bottom of my vision, my stage remained black, as the curtain never rose. In a matter of a few months, I went from normal vision to my present and future state of being totally blind in my right eye.

CHAPTER 17

As I sat in my wheelchair bent over with my face resting in my folded arms placed on the table in front of me, I hoped I wasn't in store for the same pain I had experienced once before. The symptoms were starting to repeat themselves. The initial pain was in my lower back, not centered, but a little off to the left side. It wrapped around the left side of my body and was approaching my groin. It was the same start associated with my first experience with a kidney stone.

I was hoping it was maybe something I had eaten for either lunch or dinner, or that maybe I would feel better after going to the bathroom. After another hour went by with the pain increasing and no relief from sitting on the toilet, I decided to go straight to the emergency room rather than waiting to be in total agony.

When I arrived at the emergency room and explained that I thought I was experiencing a kidney stone, they took me right in. I was shocked at how quickly I was seen, as with all my previous visits I ended up having to wait for an extended period of time. I didn't realize kidney stones ranked so high within the pecking order of emergency triage. I told myself to make a mental note should it ever come in handy in the future!

Once again, blood was drawn, urine was taken, and x-rays were requested. Sure enough, when everything came back, it pointed to a kidney stone, which could also be clearly seen in the x-ray. I was quickly given an IV and before I knew it, the pain had disappeared. I can't imagine living back in the days before modern medical technology. I had passed a kidney stone before on my own, and I wasn't about to go through that experience again if I could help it.

The urologist was able to locate the x-rays on file from my previous experience. This time around, the stone was located higher within the kidney and also appeared to be slightly larger, both signs that it would be harder and more painful to actually pass on my own. I was open to any type of procedure if it meant not having to go through equal or greater pain that I had previously gone through.

A procedure called extracorporeal shock wave lithotripsy (ESWL) was explained to me. Basically, it is a procedure that uses shock waves to smash the kidney stone into tiny pieces that can pass from the body. The urologist locates the kidney stone with an x-ray or ultrasound. Shock waves are generated and travel to the kidney area and crush the stone. ESWL is performed on an outpatient basis, and the patient can go home a few hours after the procedure. The only side effects include blood in the urine for a few days and bruising in the back caused by the shock waves. This sounded much better to me than the alternative, so I decided to give it a go.

The procedure itself went off without a hitch. I had the normal side effects, and after peeing in a cup through a strainer for a couple of days, I ultimately passed all of the shattered pieces of the original stone. The story really wouldn't be all that eventful should it end right there, but of course, I'm simply not your ordinary patient.

I went back after a week to have another set of x-rays taken to make sure all of the kidney stone had passed. The next day my urologist called, and as he was telling me that all of the stone seemed to have passed, there seemed to be some hesitation in his voice. This was good news; why then wasn't he more upbeat? It was just a matter of seconds until my excitement came crashing to a halt.

The urologist explained that he had noticed in the pictures used during the ESWL an abnormal spot located in my lower abdomen, just above my groin. At the time he didn't concern himself too much with it since he was concentrating on the ESWL and knew I'd be having more pictures taken in a week. After the new x-rays were taken and compared to the previous ones, he had some concern. The instant the word tumor came through the phone, I couldn't believe what I was hearing.

I had gone from the joy of knowing I was through dealing with the current kidney stone to all of a sudden hearing some sort of tumor had been found. Any time the word tumor comes into play, there is only one word that can follow . . . cancer!

In some ways, I was actually surprised at how composed I remained. I guess you could say since I was already living with a terminal disease, I didn't think about how many days I had left or how my daily life would be impacted. Instead, I was already in the fight mode. Mentally I already had the cancer beaten before I even knew whether or not I actually even had it.

My urologist recommended an oncologist in town and made a referral for me to see him. Through the whole process, I ended up seeing a total of four different doctors before finally making the right connection with a fifth.

I had been going to the Muscular Dystrophy clinic at The Ohio State University for years, but I never imagined I would be going to the same campus in reference to a possible cancer diagnosis. The fifth doctor I ended up being seen by practiced at the James Cancer Hospital located on the campus of The Ohio State University.

The previous doctors I had seen had all given different possible diagnoses including lymphoma or Hodgkin's disease, testicular cancer, or non-Hodgkin's lymphoma. Some wanted to go in right away and surgically remove the growth while others wanted to wait and see if it was growing. Each had their own theory, but one never seemed to agree with another. It wasn't until I was seen at the James Cancer Hospital that I felt comfortable with the plan of attack.

Even though I wasn't experiencing any of the other symptoms associated with the previously mentioned diseases, my new doctor felt it was vital to determine whether or not the tumor was benign or malignant. He said that he could go in and totally remove the growth as a couple of the previous doctors had been inclined to do, but there was a risk due to its location. The tumor was located right where my aorta splits into two arteries, each traveling down a leg, splitting like a fork in the road. It was wedged in the upside-down "V". Due to the location, there was the risk of tremendous blood loss during the surgery. Along with that risk, there would also be a long recovery period. Normally the doctor said that it takes patients at least a month to fully recover. Because of my disability and dependency on others for care, he was very cautious to give a time table.

The best plan of attack he felt was to have a needle biopsy performed to get a better reading on the growth. Tests could then be performed to determine if it was malignant, and from there the next necessary actions could be decided. The biopsy would be an outpatient procedure, and I would only require local anesthetic.

By this time, I was basically inclined to agree to any type of operation as long as it gave me a definitive diagnosis. In my head I had already gone through every type of procedure, ranging from chemotherapy, radiation, and even removal of a testicle should I have testicular cancer. I was ready to accept the challenge and knew I had the support system in place to help me every step of the way.

I'd be lying if I said there wasn't any fear inside of me. I had never heard of any one-eyed patients with muscular dystrophy who had also battled cancer! I knew there couldn't be many, and to find any survivors would be an even bigger challenge. I had plenty of friends with various forms of MD and knew of quite a few people who had gone through bouts of cancer. I also had friends who had died from both. Combining the two wasn't a pretty picture, but if anybody was ready to take it on and make headlines, I was ready. Having a form of MD has made me extremely mentally tough, so I had to be ready to take on the same mindset I had been utilizing my whole life.

I could tell the whole process had really shaken my parents. Even though I don't have children of my own, I can only imagine what it is like to see your own son or daughter suffer through any type of medical condition. Having to see your child suffer through multiple diseases is almost incomprehensible. If I was able to imagine the worst-case scenario and then picture beating it, my parents had to anticipate the worst-case scenario without me surviving; it's only natural.

The date finally arrived for the biopsy as my parents and I traveled down to Columbus, Ohio. As I went through the whole registration process and got prepped for the surgery, I felt differently than I had for any other procedure I had ever been through. I wasn't going to be put to sleep, so there weren't the anesthetic concerns. I wasn't afraid of the surgery going wrong as there were very minimal possible complications. I wasn't even concerned about the post-surgery discomfort. It was an eerie feeling. Up to that point, no diagnosis had become official. I had been battling things in my head, but no course of treatment had been set. If the tumor was found to be cancerous, what would my official diagnosis be? What kind of numbers would be put before me? How drastically would my life be altered? I had just started my first full-time job; would I be forced to quit? All of my other surgeries I could remember were to go in and fix a problem. This one was to determine how severe of a problem I had!

As I waited on the operating table for the doctor to begin, I began to look around the room at some of the equipment and tools. I thought the local anesthesia might have traveled to my head when I saw the size of the needle that was about to be stuck in my lower abdomen. I kid you not; it was the largest needle I had ever seen in my life. I tried looking in a different direction, but the size of the thing seemed to mesmerize me. There was no possible way that thing was going fit in me. The needle had to be over a foot long, and in the state of mind I was in, that foot looked more like a meter or yard stick.

I waited for the doctor to say he was ready, took a deep breath, and prepared to become what felt like being an assistant to a magician for some medieval torture illusion. Sure enough, the needle went in, and I could see the doctor make the slightest adjustments as he attempted to take a sample from the growth inside of me. With a large portion of the needle inside of me and a large portion of it sticking straight up in the air for me to see, I felt I had just become a human shish-kabob.

Going through the procedure wasn't nearly as stressful as having to wait for the results. The doctor said that it would probably take about a week, but having it stretch over two weekends made it closer to two weeks. Those two weeks felt like an eternity.

Every time my phone rang, I hesitated to see who was on the other end. As much as I wanted to know, the status quo seemed quite comforting. Finally, the phone call came, and it was time to find out how much of the status quo would actually be changing.

I thought I would be able to tell right away whether it was good or bad news from the tone of my doctor's voice. Instead, all my analyzing did was put me more on the edge as I couldn't tell where he was going. Why he didn't just come out and say so right away, I don't know, but the word "benign" finally came out of his mouth. I know I missed quite a bit of what he said next, as it felt as if the weight of the world had just been lifted off my shoulders. As happy as I was, all of a sudden I snapped out of my euphoria and realized the doctor was still talking on the other end of the phone line. I quickly grabbed a pad of paper and pen to take notes, as I knew my parents would want every last detail, and then some more.

The doctor said that part of the reason it took so long to get me the results was that he was a little confused by what he found. Being that every diagnosis in my life, ranging from my MD to my eye condition, was rare or out of the ordinary, this didn't surprise me at all. He explained the growth was due to a condition called hematopoiesis. Although hematopoiesis can take on many forms and is initially a normal part of human growth progression at birth, my growth could most easily be described as a mass of marrow that had grown outside of the bone and attached itself to my aorta.

When the doctor first read the results, he was a little confused or worried he might have stuck the needle too far in me during the biopsy and mistakenly inserted it into my spine, which would have produced the marrow. It wasn't until after going back and analyzing the results for a second time that he could confirm the sample was from the growth, and a diagnosis of hematopoiesis was made.

So, all of this information was great, but what did it all mean for me? What was the bottom line? Hematopoiesis, or the growth itself, presented no immediate danger. The only complications could occur if the growth were in fact to grow and restrict some of the blood flow through the aorta. Had I not had the x-rays taken for my kidney stone, it probably would never have been detected, as I wasn't in any type of pain or experiencing any symptoms. Basically, the doctor suggested periodically monitoring the size of the growth and making sure there were no drastic changes.

After hanging up the phone, I was in a state of disbelief. This is going to sound very weird and twisted, but I sort of had a sense of a letdown. Don't get me wrong; I was thrilled out of my mind. I really couldn't have hoped for any better news. It was just that I had mentally geared myself up so much for the worst that I didn't know what to do next. I was ready to do battle with the dragon, and now there would be no fight. Trust me; it's not like I was hoping for a diagnosis of cancer; it's just that I was ready to defeat cancer.

Looking back on the situation, it's amazing how stressful the unknown can be. Of course, the unknown can turn out to be the perceived known, which is even worse. If anything, the experience reinforced what I had already known about the medical world. It is vital to get multiple opinions.

Had I gone with any of the first four doctors I had seen, I would have been under the knife for what they felt was a case of lymphoma or testicular cancer. I hate to think what scenario might have taken place and what I'd be with or without today. As it turned out, I could take double comfort in the status quo.

CHAPTER 18

I T WAS while reading one of my disability magazines in the fall of 2000, when I came across an article featuring a wheelchair hockey league that just happened to be located in Michigan. At the end of the article was a contact number for one of the players that ran the league. A couple of days later I worked up the courage to give the number a call and inquire about the league. As luck would have it, that upcoming Saturday was an open gym/practice session, and I was encouraged to come out and give it a try. I had my doubts, as hockey had always ranked towards the bottom of my favorite sports; but to say I enjoyed myself would be a huge understatement.

People tend to think wheelchair sports are open to all those who use wheelchairs. In reality, most wheelchair sports are tailored to those who use manual wheelchairs. Due to a lack of upper body strength, power wheelchair users get left out. Wheelchair hockey, or PowerHockey as it is commonly referred to, lends itself perfectly to power wheelchair users who don't have the upper body strength to shoot a basketball or propel themselves in races. Players don't even have to have the ability to hold onto a stick, as one can be attached to a chair. By simply relying on the momentum of the wheelchair, a player can shoot or pass the ball.

A team consists of five players on the floor at one time, including the goalie. Normal hockey rules apply with a couple of changes made in order to make game play more accommodating. Deliberate checking isn't allowed, but trust me when I say that contact does occur; this isn't a powder-puff sport. All players use their wheelchairs from everyday life, so that becomes a good way of keeping contact in check, so to speak. This isn't a "just for fun" league or something simply to get people in wheelchairs out of the house. It's an opportunity to participate in a sport and release competitive juices. As the league motto states, "Don't just sit there; play hockey!"

After explaining my new hobby to friends, I kept seeing this look of confusion or disbelief on their faces. It was then that I realized I always needed to mention that the game is played in a gym like floor hockey, not on ice!

There were approximately 40 people in the league. The youngest to play was ten years old while the oldest was in his sixties. Players had all kinds of disabilities and diseases, as the only requirement was that a player utilizes a wheelchair as part of daily life.

One of my greatest memories of joining the league was simply receiving my jersey; it had my name on the back and everything else a regulation jersey would include. No longer was I the student manager on a team, the official scorer, or a referee; I was actually a member and player on a team. It had been about 15 years since my last experience as a member of a team. It didn't matter to me that this wasn't baseball. I was back into sports again!

The Wheelchair Hockey League (WCHL) added so much to my life and gave me experiences I doubt I would otherwise have been able to experience. It also taught me many lessons and made the reality of my disease all the more poignant. During my years in the league, eight players died. All eight had a form of muscular dystrophy. Some were after long hospital stays, while others were what seemed like news out of the blue. Some deaths were during the season, while others were out of season. All were too soon.

You never become immune to the effect a death can have on you, but sometimes you can become numb to the shock. Having lost those classy young men and also experienced the loss of other friends with MD whom I've known through clinics and telethons, makes me realize that even I take the simplest joys in life for granted. It makes me remember that if I'm not careful, the simplest cold can turn into a life-threatening case of pneumonia. A cough can quickly turn to fluid in the lungs and a trip to ICU with a ventilator being inserted. There's no such thing as a simple little cold or feeling just a little under the weather. Any time somebody dies, it is tragic. When it is due to a cause you've been told you could die from, it hits home. I can't say that it makes me feel like my time is running out, or it doesn't drive me harder to overcome the hand I've been dealt, but it does make me appreciate my family and friends that much more. I cherish the strength they give me and the happiness we share together. Disability or not, tomorrow is never guaranteed.

I had more than my fair share of success in the league, on an individual and team basis. I was selected to participate in the league all-star game every year I played and was named the All-Star game's MVP one season. I was voted the league's best all-around player twice, to go along with collecting an assists title. My team captured the Wheeler's Cup one season, our version of the Stanley Cup, which goes to the winning team for the playoffs. I also added the President's Trophy to my collection as I was named the MVP for the playoffs that same year. Off the court I was also recognized and received the league's leadership award. I sat on the player's governing board, rules committee, and was the league's Deputy Commissioner for two seasons. Playing wheelchair hockey was one of the greatest additions to my life. It provided that physical and mental release which had been missing for so long. While competing in the WCHL I also helped form a Power Soccer team in the Lansing area, expanding my athletic opportunities.

PowerHockey is really growing, both on a national and international level. Currently, every two years the sport holds what is known as the North America PowerHockey Championship, featuring the top PowerHockey teams from the United States and Canada. The WCHL formed a quasi all-star squad to compete in this event which I was fortunate enough to be selected to play on. Known as the Michigan Mustangs, we traveled to Calgary, Alberta, Canada for the 2006 North America PowerHockey Championships. For my whole life I had wanted to be a part of a travel sports team, and my opportunity had finally arrived. I ended up being one of our team player representatives and spent countless hours in organizing the trip. It's tough enough just trying to keep things in order and processed for a regular team traveling to a tournament, but add that we're dealing with 10 players—all in power wheelchairs, nine of whom required the help of a health care assistant or parent—and it becomes a monumental task.

Almost a full year was spent in fundraising activities to help offset the total of close to $19,000, covering player and attendant costs. We practiced as a team almost every Saturday during the summer leading up to the tournament, which was held during the first part of August. Little did I know all of my time practicing on the gym floor might have been better off spent on the sidelines with our coach working on X's and O's.

CHAPTER 19

After traveling over 1800 miles, we were only a couple of miles away from reaching our destination. That's when I saw through the bus windshield a car in front of us getting closer and closer, and we didn't seem to be slowing down a bit. I quickly looked at our bus driver who wasn't looking ahead. With a million thoughts going through my mind, yet no way to act on any of them, we crashed into the rear of the stopped car.

This trip was to be one of the major highlights of my life. I had spent nearly a year coordinating it and couldn't wait for the tournament to begin. Nine other power wheelchair users and I had been selected to represent the state of Michigan in the 2006 PowerHockey Cup.

Right from the start, when it was determined we would be competing in the tournament, I, along with one other member of the team, took the lead roles in representing our team and coordinating the whole trip. Whether it was scheduling practicing, setting up fund-raisers, or completing the necessary forms and waivers, we, along with our coach, headed things up. Every spare minute I had was devoted to make the trip happen. Getting ten power wheelchair users safely across to the opposite side and out of the country is no small task. For starters, it meant initially driving an extra couple of hours to a different airport so we could be on a direct flight without having to change planes—a major challenge for all of us needing assistance when transferring out of our wheelchairs.

As I was growing up, I had followed and watched my brother travel to compete in various games and tournaments with both school and summer teams. It's something most children get to experience, but had been a major void in my youth. My muscular dystrophy had progressed too far by the time I would have been old enough to compete at that level.

I suppose much of the reason I competed in wheelchair sports was to compensate for the void I felt as a child. I simply say that it was better to get it out of my system then, than later on try to live vicariously through the lives of a son, daughter, or college and professional athletes.

Our team ended up flying out on two separate flights per the airlines' request because one airplane wouldn't be able to store all of wheelchairs and equipment together. I ended up going on the second flight with three others from our team. Overall, there were eleven of us in our party on that flight. All the players, except for one, required the assistance of an aide, so loading and unloading on the plane took quite awhile.

The flight actually ended up being uneventful, as there were no problems. All of our chairs and equipment arrived undamaged, which is no small miracle as anybody who has flown with a wheelchair before knows. Waiting for us upon arrival was a volunteer from the tournament committee who escorted us to the area where an accessible bus was scheduled to transport us to the University of Calgary, where we, along with the majority of the other teams, would be staying.

The day before the tournament's first whistle, my adrenaline was already pumping faster than I could ever remember. In less than 24 hours, our first game was to start, and I would be competing in an international sports tournament representing my home state. This was not just some feel-good, powder-puff, social get-together event where everybody goes home a winner with a participant ribbon. This was an actual competition with winners and losers where the only tears would be from the disappointment of losing or the euphoria of winning, not from heartfelt emotions of seeing people in wheelchairs doing more than sitting at home and watching reruns of *I Love Lucy*. These stories and scores would run in the sports section of newspapers, not the human-interest section.

We got to our loading area, and our bus pulled up to the curb. The driver stepped out and tried to lower the wheelchair lift for us to board. The lift didn't seem to want to cooperate and wouldn't lower. After about ten minutes of various attempts along with multiple radio communications back to the main dispatch center, it was determined that the lift was broken and a different bus would be sent over. We didn't mind and looked at the situation as being better than had we all loaded and the lift broke with us onboard, being unable to get off!

An hour went by, and the restlessness was really starting to set in. What was taking so long? They had said it wouldn't be long for a second bus to arrive, but how long is not too long? We joked that since we were in Canada there must have been some exchange rate we hadn't taken into consideration. Unfortunately, we were in for a much longer wait as we received word that the second bus had gotten a flat tire and was out of commission, and all of the other busses being used for the tournament were scheduled to be with other teams. We were told that we would have to wait another couple of hours before one would be available for us to use. Needless to say, we became quite familiar with the Calgary airport.

Finally, more than three hours after landing, a bus arrived for us to take to the campus—one with an operating lift! The airport was relatively close to the University of Calgary, and we were told that the ride would take less than a half an hour with the current traffic. If only the ride would have been that quick.

One thing I noticed right away was the wheelchair tie-down system on the bus didn't include a shoulder strap or restraint. Upon inquiring, I got a confused look from the driver and later found out that this isn't a requirement in Canada, like it is in the United States.

It could have been a lot worse. There wasn't the sound of smashed glass or anything like you would hear in a movie. It all happened so quickly. We were literally just minutes away from our final destination, so close yet ultimately so far away. The car we crashed into looked like an accordion crunched in from behind. The rear was smashed all the way forward to the driver's seat. Had there been any passengers in the back seat, I don't see how they would have survived. Looking at the front of our bus, you wouldn't have known the damage it had just performed. Inside was a different story.

There wasn't mass hysteria, but there was a sense of panic and people yelling across the bus to see if everybody was all right. No words came out of my mouth. I heard my mom from the back of the bus yell to my dad, "John, look at Mo!"

My wheelchair had been properly tied-down to the floor of the bus, and it stayed secure during the crash. I was wearing my wheelchair lap belt, which prevented me from flying forward out of my chair. The problem was that there was no shoulder strap to keep my upper torso from being thrust forward. With my pelvis being locked in place and the rest of my body thrown forward, the whole force of impact was placed on my hips. I slammed forward like a closed clam shell.

I instantly heard two popping noises which seemed to come from my extreme lower back area; I thought I had just been paralyzed. I knew paralysis worked from the bottom of your body to the top, depending on where the fracture on the vertebrae was located. I was able to move my head and neck and quickly tried successfully to shake my hands. Next, I wiggled my toes, and since I was still bent forward with my chest in my lap looking down at the floor, I could see my feet moving. Maybe I had escaped the collision without any serious injury. That's when I tried to sit myself back up, but couldn't. It's not that I couldn't due to a paralysis or lack of strength; I couldn't because it simply hurt too much to make that movement. That's when my mom must have seen the expression on my face and screamed to my dad.

My dad ran to the front of the bus where I was located and gently helped me sit back up in my wheelchair. Looking into my eyes, he could see the pain I was in was more than just physical. Just as he had done eleven years earlier when I fractured my femur in high school, my dad was reading my mind and feeling my emotions without me saying a word. We didn't know what the extent of my injury would be, but we both knew one of my biggest dreams had just been ripped away from me just as it was about to come true.

The police came, reports filed, and it was determined rather than to try and transfer me over into an ambulance, I would stay in my chair and the bus would take me to the hospital. In retrospect, maybe I should have taken the ambulance to speed up the emergency room process.

Everybody likes the concept of free health care provided for all. I experienced the concept first hand in Canada, and let me tell you that I'm happy to be an American. For six hours I sat in excruciating pain in the waiting room. It was another two hours before x-rays were taken. It wasn't until after I had x-rays that I would be administered any pain medication. I know there are waits in American emergency rooms; trust me, I know as well as anybody, but I don't think you'll find a case where somebody has to wait eight hours to get attention after being in an auto accident and isn't able to move without extreme lower back and pelvic pain.

When the x-rays came back, the doctor diagnosed it as a crack on the left side of my hip where the femur inserts. The plan of recovery was to wait it out and let it heal on its own; not too much different from when I fractured my trochanter. The diagnosis wasn't clicking with me. I was in much more pain this time compared to my previous experience and felt there had to be more going on. After all, I had gone back in and played after my hockey fall in 2001, and now the slightest jolt or movement sent me up the wall.

I ended up being discharged early the next morning and went straight to campus to meet with my team, as they were preparing for the opening ceremonies and our first game to immediately follow. I talked with our coach who had met with the team to give them the news of my break and that I wouldn't be able to play during the tournament. He said that they were really down, not necessarily for competitive reasons, but because they were my friends and they knew how hard all of us had worked and the time put in. They were feeling badly for me.

In professional and even college sports, it isn't uncommon for a main contributor for a team to go down with an injury. Typically, you'll hear announcers commentate on how that athlete has been a positive motivator for the team and can be seen on the bench either assisting the coach or waiving a towel to cheer everybody on. You'll also hear of situations where an injured player becomes a negative factor. Right then and there I decided I would be a towel waiver and be as much of a leader as I could possibly be on the sidelines.

Unfortunately, our team couldn't pull off a feel-good story. We weren't able to qualify out of pool play to compete in the medal rounds. The accident just threw everybody off, both mentally and with game play. Our shifts and rotations were all different, and it was hard for everybody to focus. They knew I was injured, but for those who were also on the bus, I'm sure some were imagining that it could have been them.

We were scheduled to be in Canada for six days. After spending the first night in the emergency room, I spent the next night in bed in my dorm room with my parents. Let me also tell you that these were not the original rooms our team was supposed to stay in. We got relocated because there was a fire in the dorm we were going to be in the day we arrived. It was simply one more event that had toasted everybody mentally. That would also be the last time I would sleep in a bed for more than a week.

Getting up the next morning and transferring back into my wheelchair was more than I could deal with. I didn't want to have to go through that again, so I ended up sleeping in my wheelchair for the rest of the trip. The less movement I had to make, the better.

My pain had intensified so much that I went back to the hospital to get stronger medication. Seeing how much pain I was in, the doctor prescribed and wrote up a letter stating that it was in my best interest to fly back home in some type of medical airplane where I would either be able to be transported in my wheelchair or on a stretcher, so I wouldn't have to be moved into a regular airplane seat. The close quarters are difficult enough to manage when I'm not injured; I could only imagine what it would be like in my current state.

We soon realized it would be a difficult process to get approval for the medical flight from the bus's insurance agency, as they were being most uncooperative. Too bad it would only continue to get worse.

They knew they had us in a bind, as we were working against the clock. The longer they held out, the closer our departure date would get, and we'd be stuck having to take the commercial flight we were scheduled for. It was during a face-to-face meeting with one of their representatives that turned into one of the closest times I've ever come to actually striking somebody due to their insensitiveness. The representative asked me to explain why I thought I required the medical flight back home, as opposed to flying on a regular airplane. After telling her the current pain I was in, describing the assistance, movement, and trauma my body would encounter being manipulated into the limited space inside an airplane, and physically showing her the limited amount of movement I could withstand, I figured she would acknowledge my need. Not only that, but I had a doctor's statement saying the same thing. Flying on the regular flight would not only be terribly painful, but would also cause further physical damage.

She had the audacity to look me straight in the eye, deny the request and say, "I'm sorry, but it's not a perfect world." *It's not a perfect world . . . it's not a perfect world!* Here I am, sitting in a wheelchair with a terminal disease, blind in my right eye from a rare disorder that normally only strikes the elderly, just a year past being told I had cancer, unable to transfer out of my wheelchair to sleep because it caused too much pain, unable to compete in the tournament of my dreams, and SHE'S telling ME, "It's not a perfect world!" I was ready to make her world a little less perfect.

My parents must have been able to tell that I was about to fly off the handle, because they quickly seized control of the conversation and tried to get things back in order. Later on I'd find out they were just as steamed as I, but were able to contain their emotions just long enough to get through the meeting.

Without having to deny the request in writing, the insurance agency just delayed and waited for the date of our scheduled flight to arrive. We couldn't risk not going on the flight, staying in Canada, having the request be officially denied, and then ending up being stuck in Canada without any flight to get back.

There are different types of physical pain, and I think I've experienced just about all of them. There's throbbing, shooting, lingering, burning, and too many others to put into words. All I know is that I never again want to have to go through the pain I felt getting on and off that airplane. I honestly don't know how I didn't throw-up, pass out, or go into shock and convulsions.

Wheelchairs are too wide to fit down the aisles in airplanes, so what airlines do is put passengers into what are called aisle chairs to transport them to their seat if they are not able to walk to it. These aisle chairs can't be much wider than a foot in width, and you look like a NASCAR driver with the way they strap you in. Both your arms and legs are pulled in really tightly so they don't bump into anything. Your feet are also pulled back as much as possible to make the turn going down the aisle as easy as possible. I literally couldn't contain myself when they were strapping me in. I wasn't out of control or screaming like a maniac, but I was wringing wet in sweat, white as a ghost, and tears were pouring from my eyes. The crew was great in trying to help me out, but there really was nothing they could do. It was determined that the aisle chair was causing me too much pain and could only end up doing me more harm. The only way I was going to be able to get to my seat was with my dad physically lifting and carrying me to it. This was something we had done a million times over the course of my life, but never with these circumstances. It was an all-or-nothing scenario.

As physically painful and difficult it would be for me, I knew mentally it would be twice as bad for my dad. One of the toughest things for any person to do is to intentionally hurt a loved one. As twisted as it sounds, I knew my dad was the only person I could count on to hurt me and love me enough to continue to hurt me even more and make it to the seat. I don't know how we did it, and I don't even like thinking about it, but we did. In a giant bear hug, my dad lifted me, and we squeezed sideways through the tight quarters and made it to our seats. I had barely recovered when the airplane landed and then it was the same thing all over again. Somehow my dad and I got hooked or caught on something getting off, which resulted in even more jostling and thrusting before getting put back in my wheelchair. I don't know if I said more than ten words the rest of the day I was in so much pain.

As fate would have it, my parents had scheduled their move from Traverse City to East Lansing the Monday following our return from the tournament on Thursday night. Over the course of the weekend, my parents and I realized I was dealing with something larger than originally diagnosed. I couldn't manage in my current state. Besides the pain, I was also starting to have some major skin breakdown on the back of my legs and butt. I had been in my wheelchair without any prolonged type of break for a week.

On Friday I called Dr. Brophy's office. He was out of town, but I would be able to meet with one of his partners first thing Monday morning. Monday morning couldn't arrive quickly enough, and when it finally came, I was ready to get a new opinion. Of course new x-rays were required, which was not the most fun activity in the world, but I somehow managed to make it through the additional transfers and positions required to get the needed x-rays. This time, the pictures told a little more of the story. Turns out that I had more than just a simple crack on the left side of my hip. I actually had two fractures, one on each side of my hips. As bad as the news was, I was glad to be back in the USA where I could get the care and treatment I needed, not to mention the proper diagnosis.

Since my parents were literally right in the middle of their move, and with me living in East Lansing, it was determined that my case would be transferred down to Lansing where the ultimate decision would be made on my course of treatment. In what has to be one of the most emotionally draining days of my life, we packed up the final boxes into our van, said good-bye to the house I grew up in, and started the three-hour trip down to East Lansing to figure out the action plan required for my hips. Did I happen to mention it was August 14th? In a cruel ironic twist, it was the same date as my parents' wedding anniversary and exactly 21 years after the date I was initially diagnosed with muscular dystrophy.

We met with the orthopedic surgeon and talked over my various options. Every course had some risk associated with it, but the bottom line was that I was in too much pain to simply hope things would get better on their own. I decided to have surgery on both of my hips. The next day I went in for surgery and successfully had a total of two plates, three bolts, one nail, and a titanium rod placed inside me. This was in addition to the titanium rod and four screws already in my right femur from that previous fracture.

The rehab process was methodical, but I pushed forward as quickly as my body would allow. Initially I stayed with my parents in their new condo, and was able to move back into my apartment by November. My doctor had originally approved me to miss up to a year of work. I was back working part-time within two months and by the following February, I was fully discharged and allowed to engage in most everyday activities.

I still have some discomfort from the surgery in my left knee and will continue to on a permanent basis. The rod that was inserted down my left femur ended up being a hair too long, and when I extend or flex my knee, I can feel it grinding underneath my kneecap. If I were still ambulatory, they would probably remove the rod, but since I'm in my wheelchair and it doesn't cause me any pain while I'm sitting, we decided to leave the rod in place, rather than going through with another surgery. Plus it gives my hip and femur more strength.

People ask me all the time if I ended up with a big payout or any type of legal settlement. Since the wonderful experience occurred out of the country, I barely was even able to recoup all of my costs after the medical bills came in. Just my luck.

CHAPTER 20

WHAT'S IT like living with a disability? What do I wish most of all that I was still able to do? Am I in constant pain? Can I perform sexually? Do I receive any monetary assistance from the government? How old was I when I was in my accident? How do I sleep in my wheelchair? What do I want to be called: handicapped, disabled, crippled, wheelchair user, person with a mobility characteristic? This is just a small sampling of questions I've been asked at one point or another. Most of the time they are asked with sincerity, but I know there have been other situations where people have been trying to see if they can get a jolt out of me or degrade me in an attempt to boost their own self-esteem.

What's it like living with a disability? Everything that goes along with having a disability is tough. Sure, I can get prime parking spots wherever I go, but don't you think I would trade that in a heartbeat just to be able to stand and walk on my own? I can't remember the last time I was in a vehicle that didn't have the word *van* or *bus* in it. I've been relegated to driving a vehicle that's infamous for being driven by moms ten miles per hour below the speed limit with five screaming soccer kids in the back.

What's it like living with a disability? Some days are better than others, but all it takes is one wheelchair malfunction, one spilling of food, one urgent sensation of having to go to the bathroom with no accessible facility in sight, or one curb with no ramp or cutout visible, to throw reality in my face. All it takes is a stuffy nose to remind me I'm just one common cold away from it turning into a case of pneumonia and a trip to ICU. All it takes is seeing a father and son playing catch together on a warm summer day to realize I won't be able to do that. If I were to allow it, every little sight or every little sound could be a reminder of all the things my disability takes away from me. Luckily, I've been blessed to have the mindset that every little sight and every little sound is also a blessing. Maybe I won't be able to play catch with my son, but I can take him to his first game and teach him all the strategies of the game. I can be there to cheer him on and be his biggest fan. I can be the best father I can be, and love him like nothing else, just like my dad has done with me.

What's it like living with a disability? I have two constant fears in life. One is physical while the other is social. My biggest fear isn't dying from my disease, but rather dying due to choking on a piece of food or not being able to clear my lungs or air passage of phlegm. I don't have the same strength in my diaphragm to cough and clear anything in my airway, should there be any blockage, and, as previously stated, it would take some quick thinking and creative positioning to apply the Heimlich maneuver on me since I am not able to stand on my own and would be seated in my wheelchair.

My biggest social fear is remaining single for the remainder of my life. For as independent and confident as I am in daily life, I have very low self-esteem when it comes to anything dealing with dating. I want nothing more in life than to get married and have a family of my own. I can't imagine the emotions that would overflow should I see my bride walking down the aisle towards me or to be in a hospital delivery room and hear the cries of our baby entering the world for the first time.

Part of the reason I have such a hard time asking girls out is due to a few poor experiences I've encountered. More than once I've asked a girl out only to have her call me a day or two later to cancel because she was already in a relationship or just wasn't interested, but really she just didn't want to hurt my feelings in person by saying "no". I know this also happens to guys who aren't in wheelchairs, but it starts to become more than just a coincidence when it occurs multiple times. I've tried the online dating game, but that's exactly what I don't want . . . a game. I could not mention my disability on my profile or just post a picture that is a head shot, as to not show my wheelchair, but what good is that? At some point they are obviously going to find out I'm in a wheelchair. I'd rather have a girl not be interested in me right away, due to my disability, than to have her attracted by my profile and then find out later I'm in a wheelchair, and cut off communication. Even if I was into the bar scene, it's nearly impossible for me to get from one spot to another, as aisle ways are so cramped and layouts are nearly impossible to maneuver in a wheelchair.

What's it like living with a disability? No matter what, I'll always know I'm different. I'm not talking about the kind of "different" like having a big nose or funny last name. I'm talking about the kind of "different" that no matter what I do or say, the first thing people always see about me is that I am in a wheelchair. Before I even have the chance to say hi, some thought about my wheelchair has already entered their head. That's not to say it has to be a negative thought, but you only get one shot at a first impression, and mine is already done for me before I can do anything about it. How do I know this? I know it because I even find myself doing it when I see another person in a wheelchair. If I do it, and I'm in a wheelchair, I can only imagine what's going through the mind of everybody else that isn't in a wheelchair or doesn't have a close friend or family member with a disability.

When people see a person in a wheelchair portrayed on TV or in the movies, they may not have any other knowledge about or experience with such an individual. With little else to go on to either refute or support the validity of the media portrayal, these images can have a profound effect on beliefs and attitudes. This effect shows up in the form of a general lack of understanding and can add to the social barriers concerning direct contact and interpersonal communication with wheelchair users. While such images are present, they aren't necessarily accurate or helpful to the disabled community.

What's it like living with a disability? I've read all kinds of articles and stories highlighting others with various forms of disabilities, and it's quite common to read if a cure or treatment were to materialize, the person with the disability would not take it. They say that their disability or disease is part of them as a human being and is what makes them who they are. While I can see where they are coming from, I'm about as far at the other end of the spectrum as I can get. If a cure were found tomorrow, you can bet I am going to do everything within my power to be first in line to receive it.

While I do wonder what kind of person I would currently be if I hadn't grown up with my disease, I've learned more lessons in life than anybody my age should have had to at this point. I recently turned 30 years old, something I'm proud of and quite the accomplishment considering at the time of my original diagnosis, my parents were told that there was a strong possibility I wouldn't live beyond my teens. The problem is that no thirty-year-old should be looking at a birthday as an accomplishment that early in life. There's so much more I want to accomplish and do. I'm not scared of death; ironically, in order to have life, there must be death. I just want the opportunity to experience all the phases of life each and every one of us deserves to go through.

What's it like living with a disability? Beyond the physical limitations, the reason I feel it is so hard for people with a disability to succeed in today's society is a result of the poor education that takes place at an early age for all children concerning disabilities. Due to this lack of education, people with disabilities are still seen as outcasts at times and not fully accepted. They aren't given the opportunities to showcase their abilities. Early on and throughout school, children have full units during Black History Month or Women's History Month. Even though it's taboo to talk about religion, schools still teach freedom of religion and go over various beliefs from all around the world. What is taught about disabilities? Absolutely nothing that I can recall. Sure, there are the token pictures of somebody using a wheelchair here and there or maybe a person using a Guide Dog in another picture, but nothing is ever discussed or mentioned as to all the various reasons why a person may be in a wheelchair.

I get people that come up to me all the time and ask when I was in my "*accident*". Well, unless they are referring to when I was conceived by my parents, there was no "*accident*". For my parents' sake, I better clarify that; my conception wasn't a mistake. The way in which my DNA coded and reads are where the mistake or *accident* takes place. Just because I can speak clearly and don't drool, people assume I've had some kind of spinal cord injury. Not only is that an insult to me, but it is also an insult to all people that have disabilities which also cause them to drool or have impaired speech. People are naturally scared of what they don't know. By implementing early education, we could be sure people would start learning more about disabilities and becoming more comfortable around the people that have them. Unfortunately, our society still places many false stigmas on people who have a disease or disability.

Living with a disability is being a part of the forgotten minority, as I like to term it. Part of the problem lies within the disability community as a whole. The problem is that there are so many different disabilities, each with its own specific concerns and needs that we sometimes forget to work together for legislation, instead of butting heads and working against each other.

What's it like living with a disability? Prior to my current job, I went through nine job interviews. During that period, I made it all the way through to the final cut only to end up as the second or alternate choice, eight times. One time is frustrating; two times is a cruel coincidence; three times is a developed pattern; eight times is a negative reflection upon our society. It's tough knowing that when I go in for a job interview, people doing the interviewing are also doing a cost/benefit analysis calculation on me in their heads. I find myself having to remain calm and composed as questions are asked to me in a way that doesn't include the opening or closing component: *"Due to being in a wheelchair . . .",* yet it's obvious that's what it being asked. Everything else being equal, I know a job will go to somebody else unless I can show I am clearly head and shoulders more qualified for the position. Even having top references isn't enough. The bottom line is that I need to have a personal individual relationship with the person who is signing the contract or in the position to offer the job.

What's it like living with a disability? I've had people come up to me and say, "You're spoiled because you have a motorized wheelchair as opposed to using a manual wheelchair." If it were physically possible for me, I'd rather use a manual wheelchair. The reason I have a motorized wheelchair is because I don't have the upper-body strength to push myself more than a just a few feet. There are many advantages of manual chairs over power chairs. I'm not going to try to make this a *manual vs. power chair* segment, but here's an easy way to think about it: If being in a power chair is such an advantage, wouldn't all manual-chair users choose to be in power chairs?

What's it like living with a disability? It's a challenge I wouldn't wish on anybody else, yet it is a normal way of life for me. As tough as it can get, I have to keep in mind that there is somebody else who is worse off than I am.

What do I wish most of all that I was still able to do? Sure, I wish I could go out and participate in physical activities, but it's the simple things I miss doing the most. The best way I answer that question is by having people do a quick and easy experiment. I ask them to sit down in a chair and then after pausing for a second or two, I ask them to stand back up. After pausing for another second, I look them straight in the eye and simply say, "I can't do that." That usually results in a reality check and begins to show everything most people take for granted.

Am I in constant pain? No; and that is the one positive about my form of muscular dystrophy. Other than muscle fatigue, there is no pain associated with my disability. I can't imagine going through life daily in pain.

Can I perform sexually? Yes, all of my organs, including sex organs, work as any normal males would work. Once again, it is another misperception that just because I am in a wheelchair I therefore have had some sort of spinal-cord injury, which could result in a loss of sexual functions.

Do I receive any monetary assistance from the government? No; and this is another one of the biggest misconceptions people have. Since I am employed full-time, I do not receive any disability checks from the government. It doesn't matter what extra costs I may encounter or how many medical bills I rack up; since I work, I don't get any disability funds. Now, I could chose to sit at home, not work, eat chips while watching soap operas or game shows and get a disability check. I could also get better home help-care coverage, but I would rather be a productive member of society. It's a personal decision I've made with my life, but many people with disabilities choose to stay at home. I can hardly blame them due to how the system is set up and how hard it is to find an employer willing to give somebody with a disability the opportunity for a job with promotion possibilities and a reasonable salary.

Why should I lose my funding to have a home help-care provider come to assist me in the mornings and evenings just because I have a job? Shouldn't it be the other way around? Since I am contributing to society, paying taxes and putting my education to use, shouldn't I be eligible for funding as opposed to the person that is capable of finding a job and going to work but decides to stay at home and soak up the system? I could write another book on State and Federal funding and the discrepancies for people with disabilities.

How old was I when I was in my accident? Once again, I wasn't in an accident! Once we start educating people at a younger age concerning disabilities, assumptions or questions like this one won't be as common.

How do I sleep in my wheelchair? Questions like this or other ones about my daily routines usually come from young children. I get a good laugh from them at times, but realize when children ask a question like this, they honestly are confused and probably picture me in my wheelchair 24 hours a day, seven days a week. It's important to answer these questions honestly and to not make kids think they've asked a dumb question. A brief explanation as to how I get transferred from my wheelchair into my bed clears everything up. It also shows that although I need help to get into bed, I sleep the same way they do, connecting one more thing we do the same way and narrowing the divide of our differences.

What do I want to be called: handicapped, disabled, crippled, wheelchair user, person with a mobility characteristic? As far as I'm concerned, just call me Mo Gerhardt. I get so sick of this politically correct society in which we currently live. I couldn't care less as to what people call me as long as it isn't directed in a derogatory way. I know this is a huge issue for many people, so I'll honor it for them by keeping up with the current jargon of the day; but in my opinion, if you are going to value your self-worth based simply on a label, you're in for some rough times. Is my life really going to be impacted if I am called a wheelchair user as compared to a person using a wheelchair? I have a lot bigger issues to be worried about than someone's choice of word order.

The assumption that a disability has the power to imprison is powerful and knows no boundaries, but disability's power to diminish lives is nothing compared to entrenched stereotypes that must be broken.

CHAPTER 21

WILL A cure be found within my lifetime for my form of muscular dystrophy? Nobody can answer that question, but that doesn't mean I don't have the hope each and every day that some new discovery will be made. The fairy-tale ending to my story would be for Kevin to be the one to find a cure and we both live happily ever after.

In the meantime, I continue to live my life the only way I know how: I look at each day as another blessing and give 100% effort in all I do. If others see me as an inspiration, who am I to argue with that. I'm sure many of the people I've looked up to or idolized feel as if they are just doing their jobs and going about their business. In many ways, that's what makes a good role model—somebody who sees him—or herself as not setting out to be special, rather setting out to be respected and trusted.

I remember reading a quote from the great New York Yankee centerfielder, Joe DiMaggio. He was asked why he always played so hard and never appeared to take a single play off no matter if it was a meaningless game in the standings or Game 7 of the World Series. His response was, "There is always some kid who may be seeing me for the first time or last time. I owe him my best."

He didn't want that child to think he'd take plays off, nor did he want that child to think it was all right not to give 100% all of the time. Not only was he a representative for the Yankee organization, but he also was representing his Italian upbringing and heritage.

I try to bring that same approach to my life. I realize when I am out in public or at my job, right or wrong, I'm representing all others who are also wheelchair users. Every time I accomplish something, I'm chipping away one more chunk of stone of what has become a boulder blocking the path for those with disabilities. As society becomes more and more accustomed to seeing people in wheelchairs in high-ranking positions, stereotypes will be broken; but, unfortunately, there are still a few rotten apples out there that choose to be blatantly offensive to those in wheelchairs. They regard wheelchair users as outcasts or leeches on society who do not contribute, but instead bank on taxpayers' money to survive.

By nature, human beings belong as one community; but by human nature, we tend to classify ourselves, by either segregating or integrating ourselves with a particular group of people. A common yet unspoken form of discrimination against wheelchair users is the unsightliness that is commonly associated with being in a wheelchair. Since certain diseases also affect the physical appearance of wheelchair users, some people are invoked to feel a slight detest in terms of physical looks. The views and opinions of some can be categorized as plain and simple ignorance due to lack of knowledge or education. Having stereotypes and misconceptions also contributes to the ignorance at hand, especially when people have minimal contact with others in wheelchairs.

Still, there are others who are just apathetic to the situation, knowing the circumstances yet choosing not to care and evading the issues. The lack of understanding is associated with the situation as opposed to the view, where refusing to help will indirectly affect them. Most use the excuse that they have a fear of doing more harm than good, lack time, or simply have a care-free attitude.

Each day I set out to do everything within my powers not to perpetuate the stereotype associated with being a wheelchair user. My disability never hindered me from trying to achieve my academic dreams. I considered myself to be on an even playing field where my physical disability didn't impact my studies in any way. As a kid, I looked at academics as my sport, or as my way to compete. I'm a very competitive person, and with the sports playing field taken away from me, I had to find another way to compete.

I am currently an Academic Specialist for The Office of Supportive Services at Michigan State University, my alma mater, where I received my bachelor's degree in business administration and my master's of science degree in kinesiology, specializing in athletic administration. I thrive on sharing my love for the university with students and making them feel positive about themselves. It's an unbelievably gratifying feeling, something money can't buy. I love the one-on-one interaction with the students and getting to know them on an individual level. I've also taught various freshmen seminar classes focusing on diversity and social justice issues, and success strategies in higher education. I want to help them realize their dreams and to respect the dreams of others.

I recently received Michigan State University's Outstanding Faculty/ Staff Award, recognizing "remarkable contributions to creating equal opportunity and an environment of excellence." Especially gratifying for me was that the selection was based on a student's nomination. It was a totally new experience for me because it was a student that felt as though I'd impacted her life in such a positive way that she took the time to nominate me for the award. In some ways, it reinforced everything up to that point in my professional career, and it was a culmination of all my efforts.

In the fall of 2006, I received the biggest honor of my life. I was named the 2007 Muscular Dystrophy Association National Personal Achievement Award recipient. The award was announced during the national broadcast of the 2006 Jerry Lewis Labor Day Telethon. It is the highest honor in MDA's program recognizing the achievements and community involvement of people across the country affected by neuromuscular diseases. The award opened doors for me to make educational appearances and motivational speeches to area youth. I love making these appearances and hope that in the future I will have opportunities to do even more on a larger scale.

My dream is to appear on the Jerry Lewis Labor Day Telethon and tell my story. When I was younger, I felt frustrated trying to find someone with muscular dystrophy, and there were no local families to advise any of us. My parents didn't have any examples of hope to look at. Now my family is able to deliver that hope and advise other families that are entering the world of muscular dystrophy and feel as if all of their dreams have been destroyed.

Ironically, right before I was notified of my award from the MDA, I received some startling news. After some prolonged DNA testing and coding which I had undergone, I was informed I didn't have Duchenne muscular dystrophy. Instead, I had an even rarer form of muscular dystrophy called Limb-Girdle (LGMD). As somebody that tries not to be labeled, it was surprisingly hard to put into words the effect it had on me. My daily routines didn't change, nor did any of my medications. There wasn't any new therapy program or regimen I would be undertaking. Basically, the only thing that changed was the term on my medical papers and charts. Limb-Girdle can occur at any point in one's life, so it's much more difficult to place a life expectancy than with DMD which strikes boys at a very early age. LGMD is generally considered to be less severe compared to DMD, yet for some reason I was having trouble coming to grips with having a new diagnosis.

I had long been dedicated to educating myself, knowing DMD and all the latest research inside and out. In some ways it felt as if my personal identity had been stripped away from me. It's hard to come up with a parallel example, but I've tried to imagine what it would be like to find out I was adopted. Nothing would change as far as what I did each day, but at least initially, I'm sure I would feel as if I'd been living some sort of lie.

Limb-Girdle muscular dystrophy isn't really one disease. It's a group of disorders affecting voluntary muscles, mainly those around the hips and shoulders, the pelvic and shoulder girdles, also known as the limb girdles. LGMD can begin in childhood, adolescence, young adulthood or even later; both genders are affected equally. When it begins in childhood, some physicians say, the progression is usually faster and the disease more disabling. The involuntary muscles, except for the heart, which is a special type of involuntary muscle, aren't affected in LGMD. Digestion, bowel, bladder and sexual function, which are carried out by involuntary muscles, remain normal.

If you remember back to our science lesson for DMD, genes contain codes, or recipes, for proteins. Physicians classify LGMD according to which protein is missing or deficient along with whether it's dominant or recessive. All dominant conditions are labeled Type 1 while recessive conditions are Type 2. Within each Type, the specific gene or chromosome deficiency is labeled starting with the letter A. For example, I have an *alpha-sarcoglycan deficiency*, which is officially classified as LGMD Type

2D. With so many different forms of Limb-Girdle, it may come to the point in the future where the term LGMD becomes obsolete and is replaced by many more specific terms.

After having new blood and lab work done on my parents and me, I received the results through the mail, so I was the first one to sort everything out. According to the tests and DNA reading that had been done, both of my parents were carriers and my disease was due to the resulting autosomal recessive deficiency. In other words, I was no longer a random mutation, but rather a result of my parents' genetic combination.

How was I going to break this news to them? We had previously always joked about how I was an unexplained genetic case, but now all of a sudden everything could be explained. My disease and disability could be traced through both of my parents. If a scientific reason had to be given for my being in a wheelchair, the finger would be pointed at both of them. After reading the results I didn't feel this way, and still don't to this day, but how would they react? Would they blame themselves for my condition? Would they feel as if they could or should have done something to prevent my fate?

Knowing my parents, I knew the best way to break the news to them would be in person rather than over the phone. Rather than beating around the bush, I started right out by saying that I had received their genetic testing results in the mail, and the results indicated my disability was a result of their status as carriers. At first, there was a look of confusion, and then after my words seemed to get processed, I saw my mom's eyes start to get glassy. My dad didn't have the same reaction; instead he seemed to have a look of panic across his face. This wasn't going so well!

I tried to make a joke about it, but they didn't seem to appreciate the humor of the situation. What was going through their heads? How much blame or guilt were they feeling? Did they even realize what this meant genetically as far as my brother was concerned? I could tell they wanted to ask or say something, but they didn't seem able to get the words out of their mouths.

Conditions such as LGMD 2D require two mutations to show themselves. When only one gene mutation exists, it may remain undetected for several generations until someone has a child with another person who also has the mutation in that same autosomal gene. The two recessive genes come together in a child and produce the signs and symptoms of a genetic disorder. We all have many gene mutations existing within our DNA in the recessive form. These go undetected due to partners not having the same mutations. These get passed down through generations in the form of being a carrier; this was the case with my parents.

Even with both of my parents having the autosomal gene mutation responsible for my disease, there was still only a 25% chance of me being born with the condition. When looking at my brother, it was safe to assume that since he hadn't shown any symptoms up to this point in his life, he wasn't affected physically. He still had a 66% chance of being a carrier, leaving a 33% chance of being totally unaffected.

Why would David even concern himself with these numbers if he hadn't had any physical effects? They could play some importance if he were to decide to start a family. David decided to have a DNA analysis completed of his blood work. When the results came back David found out he was indeed a carrier. This resulted in Jinny also being tested and her blood work came back showing that she did not carry the same mutation.

Should they decide to get married, would this affect their decision on whether or not to conceive a child? That's not for me to say. For some people knowing the odds may sway them towards adoption, and for others, it makes no difference at all.

I've had some open and honest discussions with my dad concerning similar situations. He's said to me that had he known at the beginning of my mom's pregnancy I was going to be born with a disease that was supposed to take my life before the end of my teens, he would have wanted an abortion, but would have accepted my mom's wishes, which he knows would have been to accept the risks and follow God's plan. I don't blame my dad one bit for that statement. I've tried to put myself in that same situation where I wouldn't have had any experiences with people with any sort of disability, and I think I would have come up with the same response. Our experiences have changed him so much, that now if one of his friends were to be in the same situation, the word abortion would never come out of his mouth. It brings him to tears to think he might not have had me as one of his sons, and I can't imagine not having him as my dad. He's said to me that I'm his hero and he's learned more from me than any other person. I think you'd hear that quite frequently if you were to ask any parent of a child with a disability. It just goes to show how vital it is that we start educating people, at a much younger age than what we currently do, that sometimes having a disability is simply a difference that doesn't make all that much of a difference.

When people hear that my muscles are lacking a certain protein, they often ask, "Why don't you just eat more protein?" I get a kick out of this and feel like it would be the same thing as asking somebody who is blind why he or she just doesn't wear a pair of glasses. If it were that simple, don't you think I'd be the #1 customer for the Omaha Steaks Club? Unfortunately, eating more protein than your normal requirement has no effect on any of the proteins missing in LGMD. It's true when you eat a steak, you're ingesting many muscle proteins. Your body then breaks down these proteins into their component parts and uses them to build its own proteins. A person who lacks the genetic instructions to make these new proteins won't be able to make them, no matter how much protein is eaten.

The first person I informed outside of my immediate family when I found out about my change of diagnosis was Kevin. I felt almost guilty telling him the news. Here he had been dedicating his life to research in hopes of finding a cure for my DMD, and now I was telling him I actually had LGMD.

Kevin was as supportive and classy as ever. All he was thinking about was my general well-being, and this news was positive as far as my health was concerned. Through the whole transition period, he was unbelievable. It's amazing how much research he did on his own to assist me in learning more about LGMD. His number-one goal is still to find a cure for me, and we both realize that all research eventually will help everyone with a neuromuscular disease. Kevin is still working on ways to incorporate my new diagnosis into his research efforts.

Kevin once told an advisor, "It's the reason that I'm in science. If the disease is cured tomorrow, I would get out of the lab and go do something else. Mo's diagnosis has been the sole driving factor, and this personal motivation makes it very easy for me to get up in the morning."

EPILOGUE

11:03 P.M. I lie flat on my back in bed and stretch out as much as possible. It's the first time since I got up in the morning that I'm not positioned in a seated position. My feet are propped up on a pillow so my heels don't get a pressure sore from remaining in the same spot through the night.

I've just completed the long process of being assisted with a shower and getting into bed. The feeling of lotions on my body has never been one I've liked, but the area under my thighs and butt are coated with an extra strength cream to prevent any skin breakdown in those spots and to limit the high risk of developing pressure sores.

Lying in bed is always a time of reflection for me. Some would assume it is the toughest and most stressful or emotional part of my day. I'm totally at the mercy of the world at this time. Should an emergency of any type arise, there's no way I can get out of bed and into my wheelchair on my own; I can't even change my position enough to roll on my side.

It feels good to be out of my wheelchair. As much as it has opened new doors for me, it can be confining at times. Unless you've experienced being in a wheelchair, the closest comparison I can come up with is being strapped in a seatbelt in a car for a long road trip. After awhile you just need to get out, stretch, and walk around for a little bit. Imagine being in that car for a full day without being able to get out a single time . . . every day of the year!

The ironic thing is that during the daytime I can't stand being out of my wheelchair. I feel totally trapped and at the mercy of others if I am not in my chair. It's as if somebody has chopped off my legs. All the fears and emotions of my disease are thrown in my face, and it becomes overwhelming. Any sense of independence I've gained is instantly thrown out the window, and I start thinking of all I can't do, instead of everything I can. It's not that I want to be in a wheelchair for the rest of my life, but in my current condition, it acts as my security blanket.

Out of my chair and in bed is a different story. It's as if I'm an angel floating on a cloud in the sky. There's nothing strapping me down, no other place to be. I'm free to let my mind wander off to unchartered waters and venture to lands unexplored, either in or out of my wheelchair, depending on how my mind wants to imagine me.

It's a time to get rejuvenated. It's a time to be thankful for all I am able to do. It's a time to recognize how blessed I am to have the family and friends that are in my life. It's a time to plan out my personal schedule and pick my clothes for the next day. It's a time to laugh rather than get upset at the ignorance of a few. It's a time to recognize the willingness to assist and learn from many. It's a time to put my faith in God.

11:09 P.M. Another day has gone by. Another day of seeing people rush to get from point A to point B. Another day of not being able to recall what it feels like to take a single step on my own, yet alone run. Another day of hearing people make last-minute entertainment plans to go out that night. Another day of having to pre-plan my day before it even starts, so my home help assistant knows what time to meet at night to get me ready for bed.

Another day in the life of Mo Gerhardt.

Another day filled with hope and dreams.

I've been up for seventeen hours, and I've been blessed with another day.

What's your daily routine?

ENCORE

I T HAS been a little over three years since I completed my original manuscript. A lot has happened since the summer of 2008. I was able to take advantage of the declining real-estate market and purchased my first house. Never in my wildest dreams would I ever have envisioned myself living next door to my parents, but it's crazy how things in this world shake out. As with anything that is parent/child related, there are plusses and minuses, but I will have to say it has worked out really well.

There have been some exhilarating breakthroughs over the last few years in LGMD2D research with Dr. Mendell leading the way. In April 2009 Dr. Mendell published results utilizing gene therapy, which were the first ever to show promise beyond safety alone in a human trial. No adverse events, such as rejection of the therapy by the immune system, occurred during the trial. All trial participants produced four to five times the amount of alpha-sarcoglycan protein in the gene-injected foot muscle compared to the corresponding muscle on the other foot. Participants were evaluated at six, seven or twelve weeks. Improvement in function wasn't expected from the trial due to the injection being into a very small area. A delivery method that reaches a large muscle area is necessary to improve function.

In October of 2010 Dr. Mendell published further findings showing sustained protein production six months after injection of the genes into the foot muscle. The next step in LGMD2D gene therapy is to deliver the alpha-sarcoglycan gene to an entire limb, via the blood stream. Dr. Mendell has an MDA grant to pursue this type of gene therapy for this disease.

"The overall favorable findings in this clinical trial lay the foundation for further gene therapy steps that can be taken for LGMD2D patients," reports Dr. Mendell. "The study opens the door for potential safe and effective delivery of the sarcoglycan gene through circulation."

I took a job with a different department at Michigan State and really love my new position. I'm advising for the College of Natural Science, primarily working with premed/preprofessional students. I'm also the liaison with Student-Athlete Support Services on campus. I've never had co-workers that advocate for me as much as my current colleagues. It has really renewed my faith in the human spirit. Rather than having to always feel like the whistle blower, my boss has taken a leading role in making the work environment as inclusive as can be. I've come to realize that respecting and enjoying colleagues is even more important than a job description. My previous position had gotten so toxic that my friends were telling me that it was starting to affect my disposition outside of work. That's when I really knew it was time for a change.

My biggest professional breakthrough came when I was hired by the Spartan Sports Network as the women's basketball radio analyst. The experience has been so fulfilling as it has allowed me to work in intercollegiate athletics which has always been a goal of mine. This fall will be my third season alongside my partner Rick Berkey. I can't even begin to tell you how great a partner and mentor Rick has been to me. He had been doing games all by himself and had every reason in the world to resent my joining the broadcasts. Instead he welcomed me with open arms and the two of us make quite the radio team.

In 2007 Suzy Merchant was named head coach for the MSU women's basketball program. Suzy just happens to be from Traverse City and our families have numerous connections. As soon as she arrived on campus I made sure to go in to see her and congratulate her on her hiring. I'd frequently drop in to see her throughout the year and it was great to reconnect. I was able to open up to Suzy about some of my frustrations concerning my previous job and also my difficulties breaking into the mainstream world of athletics as a person with a disability. It was during one of these conversations that Suzy told me a story I will never forget.

Along with basketball, Suzy also played volleyball in high school. There is one day from her playing career she will always remember. It was just about time for practice to start and she was bumping a ball around with some of the other girls when her coach came in. He was sort of an old-school coach who believed in the benefits of structure, routine and hard work. He'd be sure to give praise when it was merited, but he wouldn't be considered the rah-rah type. That's what made this practice even more memorable. After walking in, he called the team over for what Suzy thought would be instructions for the first drill. The team gathered and after a couple awkward silent seconds, her coach started to cry. He started to say something about his son, but then began to cry even harder. A few more seconds went by and he was then able to explain that his youngest son had just been diagnosed with a rare disease and the doctors had said that he would be lucky to live to see his twenties.

There was something about the raw emotions Suzy's coach was showing at that moment in time that stuck with her. That experience taught her being part of a team is also being part of a family. Her coach was breaking down in a way that maybe he wasn't able to do at home because he needed to show optimism and strength for his son. He was proof that heartbreak can invade even a seemingly perfect life in an instant. Support can come in many ways, and in time that team of high school girls provided a sanctuary for that coach to let out his fears and heartache. Suzy said she learned and promised herself that no matter how much success she would find in athletics, she would always remember to love and cherish her family, friends and life and be sure to give back to others.

The reason it meant so much to me to hear this story is because that volleyball coach was my dad and I am that boy. I was in second grade and Suzy was in high school, yet that one day forever linked the two of us together. As tough as it was to hear of my dad's pain and sorrow, it also gave me great comfort to know that he had another family providing him love and empathy. As much as he was a pillar of strength for me growing up, those girls were his support.

That pillar of strength took a big hit at the start of 2009 when my dad was diagnosed with prostate cancer. This was a whole new experience for me as far as somebody else in the family receiving scary news about health as opposed to receiving it myself. I have to be honest; I think it is harder to hear about a family member's diagnosis than your own. While I've grown accustomed to living with and battling my own disease, this was completely out of my hands.

It was a difficult ordeal for my dad, both physically and emotionally. My dad is a natural worrier, perceiving the unknown as scary. I tend to look at it as an opportunity. So it wasn't too surprising to see my dad struggling mentally leading up to his surgery. Thankfully, his robotic surgery turned out to be successful and he has been cancer free ever since.

Looking back on the morning of his surgery there was some Gerhardt humor. David and Jinny had come into town and we were all gathered around my dad in his holding room prior to surgery. As the nurses were wheeling his gurney away Jinny gave him some last words of encouragement saying, "knock 'em dead!" I couldn't believe what I had just heard and quickly turned to Jinny in an attempt to pull back the words that had already been spoken. The look on her face was priceless as the realization of what she had just said resonated in her mind. Of course before either one of us could say something else, my dad was already across the room and out the door to surgery.

Jinny wasn't trying to be sarcastic or anything like that. She honestly meant well and just didn't think that my dad would take those words literally. After recovering from surgery I brought it up with my dad to see if he had heard Jinny's last words. Of course he had and it was all he could think about until the anesthesia kicked in. The only thing that really shocked me was that it was Jinny who said it and not my mom!

Being diagnosed with cancer took a lot out of my dad and I'm still not positive he is 100% mentally recovered from the whole experience. One of the few times I've recently seen my dad with the smile I am used to has been while he's holding his new grandson. Yes, my brother and Jinny got married back in the summer of 2009 and just recently had their first baby, a boy named Kellen Matthew on June 4, 2011. In some ways the marriage just seemed like a formality given how long they had been together, but it was great officially welcoming Jinny to the family. I was so touched when I found out Kellen's full name. They knew beforehand that they were having a boy, but kept the name a secret until after he was born. I could tell it really moved my parents as well. I still hope to one day have a family of my own, but if that doesn't come to be, being an uncle is the next best thing.

Kellen Matthew was born just after midnight early on a Saturday morning. It was part of a weekend that I will never forget. As soon as I had heard of the pregnancy I envisioned our whole family being at the hospital in the waiting room, with my brother coming out announcing the birth just like you see on television. Unfortunately, life isn't like television as I wasn't able to be in Chicago. As luck would have it, I was committed to being in Traverse City for the weekend. I, along with three others, was being inducted into the Traverse City Central High School Hall of Fame. It's a tribute that means a great deal to me.

I had been notified of the honor a few months prior, so I was aware of the possible date conflict for quite some time. As much as I wanted to be there for the birth, I also couldn't afford to have Jinny be all that late with the delivery either; as if I had a say in the matter. I had one week free after her due date, otherwise I would be unable to take vacation until the end of July because of work demands during freshman orientation at Michigan State.

I had talked with David and Jinny on Thursday night, prior to heading up to Traverse City on Friday and told them to text me when the baby was born even if they thought it would be right in the middle of the induction ceremony. That request would come back to haunt me.

My parents had decided to be in Traverse City for the event as there was no guarantee the baby would be born and Jinny's parents were right there in Chicago for support. Plus, being on the in-law side, they didn't want to be overly intrusive. I had to be at the ceremony early, so my parents were still getting ready when my mom received a phone call from my brother saying that they were at the hospital and the doctors were keeping Jinny as she was beginning to go into labor.

The induction ceremony opened up with a reception so when my parents arrived they were obviously excited and wanted to share the news me and others. I was occupied with other guests, but of course exciting news travels fast and it wasn't too long before I found out through friends that Jinny was in labor.

Once the formal ceremony started, I was the first person up to give my acceptance speech. I always keep my cell phone clipped to the front strap of my seat cushion. That way I can just keep it on vibrate and I feel when I get a phone call without having to have the ringer turned on. Literally ten seconds into my speech I felt my phone start to vibrate. My focus changed like a dog spotting a squirrel. I had purposely left it on in case David was to text me. I never thought about how much it would throw me off during my speech.

See, ever since college when I have had to give a speech, I have memorized it. Being in a wheelchair I can't fit behind a podium and reach the microphone. If I'm holding a microphone that only leaves me one hand to hold a speech or cards and it is very awkward and difficult for me. I learned early on that memorization was the best route. I've also learned that is how I give my best speeches. It really allows me to make eye contact, connect and feed off of the audience. I got that tip from my high school band director, who always memorized our sheet music for performances because it allowed him to do the same thing with our band.

It's rather ironic that the only time I have lost my train of thought and forgotten a speech was when that very same high school band director was in the audience. My carefully memorized lines temporarily scattered like Scrabble tiles as my phone vibrated, diverted my thoughts immediately to David and Jinny. Luckily I am a good speaker and was still able to pull off a quality speech. The unfortunate thing was that I failed to mention a few specific people that I so dearly wanted to acknowledge. What made it even more frustrating was that after my speech was done and I was able to look at my phone, the message wasn't even from David!

My speech must have been better than I thought because I was asked to represent the inductees and speak to the senior class two days later at their graduation ceremony. I gladly accepted the honor and soon realized that it was going to be fifteen years to the week since I gave the speech as Senior Class President to my graduating class in 1996. I would be on the same stage in Kresge Auditorium at Interlochen Center for the Arts where our high school always held its convocations. It was a beautiful day and glorious way to conclude a weekend that will always rank near the top of my favorites. The next day I was heading to Chicago for a week to meet my new nephew with his ten little fingers, ten little toes and a loud cry!

A month from now I will be turning thirty-four. Twenty-six years ago had that been said to my parents and doctors they would have considered it a miracle. I don't consider myself a miracle and I really don't think of myself as defying the odds. What I do believe is that I still have bigger and better things ahead of me. Come May of next year, I will have spent half of my life in a wheelchair. My wheelchair has become part of me, yet it doesn't define me. I embrace it for what it allows without dwelling on its drawbacks. It's allowed me to gain insights aplenty about the true meaning of family and confronting physical and mental hurdles. It gives me perspective on what's important in life even if that perspective is from an electric chair.

I'll always be motoring forward and no matter what, I know that I will never walk alone.

Ready to take on the world at the age of three months.

Playing T-Ball for the Legal Eagles in the summer of 1985
just prior to my diagnosis.

With Mandy Berden having our picture taken before going to our Jr. Prom. I had been discharged from the hospital after breaking my leg just a few hours earlier. Notice my shorts.

One of my all-time favorite pictures with my dad. I'm in my letter jacket during my senior year prior to a baseball game. I was never able to play for my dad, but he'll always be my coach.

Kevin Sonnemann, his then girlfriend Emily Koster and I take in a baseball game at Wrigley Field in Chicago. If you look closely you can see I'm wearing my Baltimore Orioles hat.

The whole family, including our dog, Ripken, on our front porch for our 1999 family Christmas picture.

Working on the "Up" and "Get" command with Ted at Canine Companions for Independence Team Training in Delaware, OH.

Graduating from Michigan State University with a Master of Science degree in 2002. Ted walked through the ceremony with me in his own cap and tassel.

Rick Berkey and I sitting courtside at a Michigan State women's basketball game, conducting the radio broadcast.

Holding my nephew, Kellen Matthew Gerhardt, in July of 2011, less than two months after he was born.